BES

MW01042005

Cover photos by Christoff Thornborrow
Illustrated by Sam Turton
Edited by Ed Rodgers
Design & in-house editing by Joe Blades

Printed and bound in Canada

Cataloguing in Publication Data

Mouradian Ted, 1948-

 Best in life

 ISBN0-921411-55-3

1. Interpersonal relations. 2. Self-actualization (Psychology)
I. Title.
BF637.S4M68 158.2 C97-950027-3

published by
Maritimes Arts Projects Productions
BOX 596 STN A
FREDERICTON NB E3B 5A6
CANADA
ph/fax 506 454-5127   e-mail: jblades@nbnet.nb.ca

BEST

in

LIFE

by

TED MOURADIAN

To Dolores & Elie

Best in life

Maritimes Arts Projects Productions

Fredericton • Canada

TO JORDIN, BRODIE, FEIA AND CLARA
Thanks for being there for me.

TO TROY
It is my honor to be able to share this life journey with you.

SPECIAL THANKS TO
Tom Balint
Chris Cardy
Millie Cowing
The Crawford Family
Trent Crick
David Glen
Val & Rusty Kruty
Brent Kurliak
Christina MacNaughton
Fran Mouradian
David Overhold
Chris Owens
Jean Puttock
Doan Nguyen/Peter Hackley
Darcy Perron
Jean Redekopp
The Tuck Family
Mary Wakil
The Wickens Family
Jane Lynne Wilson
for having faith in me and this book.

BEST in LIFE

THE JOURNEY BEGINS

If there were only four things I could have you know, they would be these:

Each event in our life is the result of our relationship with ourselves, others and the planet.

We manage our relationships by choosing how we react to each event.

Correct reaction stems from an inner balance of spirit, mind and body.

Inner balance brings harmony to our relationship with ourselves, others and the planet.

Gaining an understanding of these four steps is what this book is about. It is a journey to the BEST *in* LIFE.

BEST IN LIFE

Let me introduce Humphry the Camel. I created him in 1986 as sort of a mascot or alter ego for my sales training and motivational speeches. Since then, as I learn more and more about camels, Humphry has become an allegory for our journey through life.

The camel, you see, has three traits that make it stand out from other animals and when we learn them, these three traits can be the starting point for all our relationships.

Here's how:

> When all the other beasts of burden fall by the wayside, whether they die or quit, the camel pays no heed. It doesn't matter how violent the weather, how difficult the terrain or how heavy the load, the camel starts and finishes. This is reliability.

That's how we should be as humans: RELIABLE. If someone asks us to do something, and we agree, we must finish the job. To our loved ones, family, friends, co-workers, we must be reliable. Every living thing on this earth should be able to count on us.

The second trait is DIGNITY.

While most beasts of burden look broken, depressed, or as if they're starving for a better lot in life, the camel stands with its head held high. It is saying to itself: "I know I'm just a beast of burden, I know I just carry someone else's load in life, I know I'm not the best looking and I know I'm not the president of a company. BUT one thing I know for sure. I am the best camel there is. As long as I am treated right, I'll do the best job possible. Treat me poorly and I'll stop and spit."

DIGNITY

Camels are proud of their existence. They know they contribute to the rest of the planet. No one has the right to yank your chain. No one has the right to discriminate or put you or any other creature down. It doesn't matter whether you are old or young, tall or short, fat or skinny, whether you are bald, handicapped, black, white or Asian, or whether you are straight or gay. Your race, religion and sexual orientation don't matter. Go through life with dignity. No one has the right to make you feel inferior in any way.

The third trait about the camel, and a really neat one at that, was shown to me by Dan Kilgariff, from Alice Springs, Australia, home of some very famous camel races. Dan pointed out that the camel's feet are very large and padded. Whenever it travels, the camel walks very softly and doesn't damage or destroy anything in its path. It bends grass, it doesn't break it.

Like the camel, as we journey through life trying to make our mark, we must be very careful not to leave a path destruction in our wake. It is much better to STEP SOFTLY with nature than to rush through life leaving behind a trail of hard feelings, hurt relationships and horrible memories.

Remember: Be reliable in everything you do, go through life with dignity and step gently. Don't let destruction remind others of your presence.

These are the keys to control your life. Fortified within, you can master the relationships without.

MY IDEAS

In the following pages, I'll delve deeper into our personal relationships and I'll explore our connections with our spirit and our loved ones. Later on, I'll touch on the relationships created by our professional lives.

As I share my ideas and philosophies on life and relationships, I'll use my own life experiences and the experiences of others I have met over the years. Everything in this book reflects my own personal conclusions, except where attributed.

I have been able to attain peace with myself and a oneness with my surroundings. This has given me a better understanding of all my relationships — personal, corporate and spiritual.

My hope is simple; that people will use these insights to live in harmony with themselves, with others and with the planet as a whole. And if we all do, the planet will be a better place for all of us to live.

I am working on a degree in life. And the learning never stops.

We are responsible for our own lives, our own actions and our own journeys. Hopefully, my philosophies, and Humphry's, can help you with your journey.

OUR SCRIPTING

I believe that when we are born we are basically good and happy and filled with a kind and caring spirit. There are many ideas on how our spirit picks our bodies or how we are created. I don't propose to argue for any of the various philosophies, but I will say that as long as your beliefs do not adversely affect others on this planet, you are in harmony. As soon as you forcefully inflict your philosophy or belief system on anyone or anything, you are in conflict with the harmony of the planet and you are affecting the relationships of others.

As we grow and develop, we are inundated with all sorts of rights and wrongs, goods and evils, yeses and nos. Most of this propaganda (yes, propaganda) is self serving. As a developing child, most of our programming comes from our parents and peers. They're sharing their standards to draw us into their belief system.

I don't say this is entirely wrong. Just as all creatures are taught to survive, so must we as humans be given the basics for a healthy life. The line must be drawn, however, when the teachings are to the detriment of other living creatures. I'm not talking about the use of plants and animals for food, but it is not right to massacre for pure sport or for religious belief. "My God is better than your God," or "Let us just kill it to see what happens," are terrible arguments for harmonious relationship management.

HUMANS ARE THE
ONLY CREATURES ON
EARTH THAT DESTROY
THEIR OWN KIND
SIMPLY BECAUSE ONE
PERSON DOESN'T
SHARE THE SAME
BELIEFS AS ANOTHER

Sometimes I think I would hate to be an alien landing here. I'd probably be shot dead because I was different before someone bothered to find out if I was friendly.

Don't get me wrong! I'm not trying to start out on a low note or lash out at anyone, but, unless we realize and understand who and what we are, it will be difficult, if not impossible, to reach harmonious relationships.

As I said before, we are all basically good, loving and caring creatures. So how can we, as thinking and reasoning beings, help harmonize the planet?

It's simple:

LET EVERYONE DO WHATEVER THEY WANT AS LONG AS THEY DON'T ADVERSELY AFFECT ANYONE ELSE

Think about it. If it isn't hurting you, if it doesn't injure others, it isn't any of your concern. Of course, the actions of others can be a curiosity or a learning process to help you better understand how you can get the best from life. But remember, just because someone believes in a different God, or has a different colour of skin, or has a different sexual orientation, you do not have the right to be judge, jury and executioner.

The only limit to freedom is the detrimental effect on others. Pursue your goals and accept no censure, as long as the impact of your actions is positive.

LOVE IS UNCONDITIONAL

In most teachings, God is love. Love, to be the ultimate love, is unconditional. We humans are funny. How many times do we fall in love with someone only to try to change them because of our own insecurities and phobias?

I don't have all the answers, but if I can get you to think about your relationships in a different light, I'll be happy.

When dealing with another life, especially a child's (for they are our hope for the future) try to share, understand and get to know them as best you can before putting yourself in a position of judgment. A lot of our decisions are based on what we believe to be right and not what is good for the other being in the relationship.

I'll use a cartoon for an example:

> Three children sit under a tree. One wears mittens. The caption reads: "Every time my parent's hands get cold, I have to wear these mittens."

Why is this cartoon so telling? Is it because:
- If "you" feel cold, we all should?
- If "you" feel frightened, we all should?
- If "you" feel inadequate, we all should?
- If "you" hate a certain race, we all should?
- If "you" love a certain type, we all should?

Martin Luther King said: "A heart can only love another heart." WOW! How simple! How true! Why do we try to destroy the beauty of that simplicity?

I'll tell you a story:

When my eldest daughter, Jordin, was 12, she was on the telephone with a boy named Corey. She was very excited. When she hung up, Jordin told me she had been trying to get Corey to call all year. Jordin said they were going together now. At 12, that means they hang around together during school and call each other afterwards. (That's all they do. I checked.)

When I asked who Corey was, Jordin said, "You know Cory. You met him on the ski trip. You know, Dad, the cute boy with curly hair. Come on, Dad, you remember."

I said, I didn't, but did she have a picture?

Jordin found her class picture and pointed to Corey. He was the only black person in the picture. Boy, did I learn something fantastic about my daughter. Not once in her description did she use the word "black." All she saw was Corey — NO COLOUR — just a boy she was attracted to.

Jordin made me proud of her that day, and I know my other daughter, Brodie, thinks the same way. It makes you feel real good!

Wouldn't it be nice if all we could see was another human being and not colour, race or sexual orientation.

That incident was one of the turning points in my life. That was the day I knew my daughters could accept my deep, dark secret. You see, I know what it's like to be discriminated against. I have a concept of what it would have been like to be a black in Mississippi in the early 1960s.

I realized some years ago that I am gay. Yes, homosexual. But wait. Don't turn off and don't stop reading. This isn't a book about homosexuality. It is a book about relationships, a book about sharing this planet harmoniously with all other living things.

Sure, I'll use some of my life experiences. They illustrate that I live and breath my philosophy. The things I write aren't textbook studies. They're real. They're not Freudian. They're not Jungian. They're pure Mouradian.

OUR PERSONAL RELATIONSHIP

OUR PERSONAL RELATIONSHIP

Of all our relationships, most important is the one we have with ourselves. Are we happy with who and what we are? It may sound like a superficial question, but if we aren't happy with ourselves how can we enjoy a successful relationship with others?

DO SOMETHING FOR THE PERSON YOU LOVE MOST

Give yourself a big hug. Love yourself first. If you can't, you don't have the capacity or understanding to love someone else or even the ability to accept love. A person who showers love on others without the self-respect to love themselves, makes me wonder how true that love is.

Some of us tend to believe, or unwittingly trap ourselves into thinking that the only way to love or get love is to lose our identity for others, to sacrifice our being for that of others, to be humble and totally give ourselves to others. That sounds great for the recipient, but what about the giver? Think of this: If you don't love yourself first, if you don't take care of yourself so that you are happy, you won't be able to help make others happy.

People with low self-esteem don't make good partners in a relationship. They don't make good employees or good friends, either. I don't want to see endless egoism, just plain old love.

I love me. I have too. I can't change who I am and I refuse to walk through life as a morose blob of depressing human flesh. I'm not perfect, but my imperfections make me unique. Each person's differences, and our acceptance of them, lets love flow back and forth — no strings attached.

Love you and you will be able to give and accept the love of others.

One way I try to re-enforce a love of myself is to do something for myself everyday. For one hour each day, I do something for Ted. This is a time that no one dictates. Whether it is sleeping, reading, running, writing or just plain meditating, it is what I want to do for me for one hour each day.

Sometimes this means getting up an hour earlier than usual or firmly separating myself from those around me, but it is important and it's worth it.

"That may be all right for you," you say, "but I have a family that counts on me. I have a demanding job. I have no time for me."

My answer starts with a question, "If you don't have time for you, why bother being you?" You do what you do for a reason. You don't do it all for others. If there is no personal reward, how can you expect to show commitment? Looking after yourself is a sure way to feel even greater love for others, to enjoy your job because it gives something back. Hamsters have hamster wheels. We have the keys to the cage.

My priorities rank like this: First, Ted. Second, family, friends and loved ones. Third, my job. There's a logical reason. If I do everything to make Ted happy first, I can make others happy.

In turn, happy friends and family will make me happy. And if I take a job that brings happiness, then I'll do the best job I can and my employers will be happy. It's a full circle.

But the only way to begin this unbroken circle of happiness is through love, love of yourself.

> *Alas is the man who can sing*
> *And dies with the song still in him.*
> — Ralph Waldo Emerson

RESPONSIBILITY

One of Humphry's philosophies is to tackle life with dignity. Humphry knows he isn't the best looking of creatures, or fastest or smartest, but he's proud of being the best camel he can be.

Always remember that YOU have control over YOUR life and that YOU are totally responsible for YOUR life. We make ourselves happy or sad, we make ourselves feel superior or inferior. A good start to mental health is to keep in proper perspective the emotions we demand from others for ourselves. We can't ask others to make us happy.

We all do have a song in us and if we learn to sing in our own special way, the song will come from deep within the love in our hearts. We will be able to share that song with people we come in contact with:
- We all have the right to sing our song.
- We all have the right to be the person we were meant to be.
- We all have the right to be happy.

HAPPINESS IS A DECISION

If our lives are in our own control, how do we become angry, sad or frightened? And how do we become happy and healthy? Some studies show we're born with personality traits, that genes are responsible for a certain part of our being. Other studies show we're influenced by outside forces such as our families and our peers. No doubt we are a combination of both, but most of all, we control our own lives. We're in charge. Happiness is a decision.

PACK YOUR OWN LUNCH

Picture a park bench in a pleasant field. Seated are two workers having lunch. The first opens a neatly packed lunch box and pulls out sandwiches with the crusts cut, a nice nappy, a vase with a little flower, some fruit and juice and a scrumptious piece of cake.

The second unrolls a crumpled paper bag. It holds a dried peanut butter sandwich.

"Oh, no. Peanut butter again," he says.

"Well," says the first. "Would you like some of mine. I have plenty."

The offer is declined and the second person eats his dry sandwich.

The next day, it happens again. The well-prepared lunch is displayed and eaten by the first person. The second person complains about the boring peanut butter sandwich and then swallows it down.

The scenario continues all week.

Finally, on Friday, the first person opens up another fabulous lunch. The second looks into the crumpled lunch bag and moans, "Peanut butter again."

"Listen," says the first, "all week all I've heard was 'Peanut butter again. Peanut butter again.' Why don't you get the person you live with to make you something different?"

The second person says, "I live alone. I pack my own lunch."

Remember, we control our own lives. What we pack, we eat.

Perhaps it will be difficult to change some of our really deep scars, but I assure you it isn't impossible.

THE PAIN OF STAYING THE SAME IS GREATER THAN THE PAIN OF MAKING CHANGE

When we change ourselves, influencing our children and others in a positive manner will be much easier. Remember that part of who we are today is the result of others' opinions and standards given to us as we grew up. We feel the way we feel about ourselves and others because of how we were programmed at an early age. In some measure, what we believe about ourselves and others is our reaction to what was put into our heads, overtly and subliminally.

Think about how you talk around your children and the tone of voice you use when you relate different things to them:
- "Don't touch yourself there."
- "Ugh. That's Kah Kah. Bad. Bad."
- "Those people aren't nice people."
- "Little boys don't do that."
- "Little girls don't do that."
- "You're too young for that. Wait until you're 18."
- "You're too old to be playing that game."
- "How could you be so stupid?"
- "Those people don't believe in the same things we do. Don't associate with them."

I could go on and on. And so could you. So think about how you relate to your children and friends.

Growing up is a learning experience. All we try to do, if we channel our energy right, is to be the best, to get the most from life. We learn through trial and error. I don't believe people in general are bad. I think they're just trying to do their best within the skills they learned as they were developing.

Maybe you're wondering how this relates to our personal relationship, our relationship with ourselves. It's simple:

HOW WE'VE BEEN TREATED AND HOW WE FEEL ABOUT OURSELVES DETERMINES HOW WE TREAT OTHERS

We have the ability to change our relationship with ourselves by changing the way we view this planet and the people on it. For many, taking control will require a great amount of time and effort. Taking control will only require small adjustments for others.

WE ARE UNIQUE
NO OTHER CREATURE IS MADE
EXACTLY LIKE US

No one can feel the way we feel at any given moment. Sure, others have been in similar circumstances and therefore have had similar feelings. We can even use the experience of others to help us decide how to act in certain situations. But we are unique. In fact, we go out of our way to establish our own identity. It always intrigues me how we try our best to be individuals yet work hard to dress and act to fit in. We don't want to be looked at as different, yet we want to be treated as unique.

I looked up "normal" in a dictionary:

> norm: n. a rule or authoritative standard; a unit for comparison; a class-average test. -a n. a rule, pattern, or standard; -al n. conforming to type or natural law; the standard; the average. -alcy n. normality. normality n. normal state or quality. -ly adv. -ative a. setting up a norm; regulative.

See. Nowhere in this definition are the terms right or wrong. Not fitting the pattern, not conforming to a standard does not imply that who you are, or what you are doing, is wrong.

It seems to me that when we try to verbalize what we think should be appropriate behavior, we tend to approach from the negative and say that anything abnormal is wrong. Is it because of our own insecurities that we fear anything different, anything that challenges the norm, anything that slips outside the usual pattern?

What is normal to one culture easily can be classed as abnormal to another. It isn't to them, I assure you. What was normal behavior 20 years ago might be classed as abnormal behavior today. Conversely, what might be abnormal today could be, and often is, normal in the future.

THE 2% SOCIETY

Don't be pummeled by the nay-sayers. We are a two percent society. We react to the two percent of negativity around us and try to classify that as the norm. A customer shoplifts and all customers become suspect. But if a customer is honest or extra warm, they're considered strange or abnormal. We don't say all customers are good.

What I'm saying is "relax." Be who you are, who you were meant to be. It is often the person who tests the edge, who breaks the norm, that helps push our civilization as fast as it can go.

It is far easier to conform than to be different. It takes energy, courage and a strong set of values to stick to what you believe.

Thoreau wrote:

IF A MAN DOES NOT KEEP PACE
WITH HIS COMPANIONS, PERHAPS
IT IS BECAUSE HE HEARS A
DIFFERENT DRUMMER. LET HIM STEP
TO THE MUSIC HE HEARS,
HOWEVER MEASURED OR FAR
AWAY.

When we have a healthy relationship with ourselves, we will realize that it doesn't matter what clothes we wear, where we live or what kind of car we drive. As long as we're happy with our station in life, what we do is OK.

The same thing is true with our physical being. Our weight, height or colour really don't matter as long as we are happy and comfortable with ourselves. Just because an advertisement shows us beautiful, lithe, athletic models, that doesn't mean it's right for us.

Why wear uncomfortable shoes? To make our friends happy? It simply invites resentment and sore feet. The secret is to dress comfortably and act in a way that will enhance your relationship with you. Ultimately, your confidence and comfort will strengthen your relationships with others.

Way back, when we were in school, the teacher would put a chart on the blackboard. Above one column the teacher would write NEEDS, above the other WANTS.

The needs column was very short: shelter, sustenance and warmth. Everything else fell under wants: life's bonuses that we can pursue with as much vigor as we deem suitable. Perhaps that lesson was so long ago, we've all forgotten. Consider how lucky we really are already.

Remember, celebrate your uniqueness. Only one of you was made and that is something special. Yes, there are certain things we have to do to conform to society. But don't ever let your specialness be smothered by the concept of normal.

WE ARE RESPONSIBLE FOR OUR OWN LIVES
DON'T BLAME OTHERS
FOR WHO OR WHERE WE ARE

Pointing fingers is easy, and the worse the situation the easier it gets. But responsibility is ours. It may seem the harder of roads, but the pay off is fantastic. By taking responsibility, we can control our lives. Control of our lives gives us our own destiny.

If you fail an exam, don't blame the teacher. Blame your study habits or avoidance of extra help.

If you trip over something at home, don't blame the person who left it there. Blame yourself for not watching where you were going.

If you are heavier than you want to be, don't blame seductive television ads or catchy packaging. Blame your eating habits.

If you get drunk and then sick, don't blame the company you drank with. Blame yourself for overindulging.

There's a bottom line here:

NO ONE IS ACCOUNTABLE
FOR OUR ACTIONS EXCEPT OURSELVES

Even with all of this, I know actions aren't painted black and white. There are shades of gray. In our upbringing, and perhaps in some of our own incorrect conclusions, other people and incidents helped form some of our mind-sets. Yet, I truly believe that when we realize our responsibility for ourselves we will become masters of our own lives. Remember the peanut butter sandwich.

LOOK TO THE LIGHT, NOT THE SHADOWS

Each of us presents to others what I call a light side or a dark side. Call it optimism versus pessimism or positive against negative. No matter the name, it is a reflection of the way each of us view the world.

More than anything, we are what we think. Our thoughts mold us. They determine our actions and limits. The dark side, likely from habit, is very persuasive. In the paragraph above, I wrote light before dark, positive before negative. The first time I put it on paper, however, it came out dark side/light side; negative against positive. My natural inclination, my first reflex, was to put bad before good.

It takes a lot of self-control to reverse the order. But there's good reason to keep a watchful eye. The light side tames all the distressing things that can happen to us. The dark side invites those very complications we worry about in the first place.

Humphry has made acquaintance with a fellow beast of burden named Jack, who belongs to that relation of horse that makes his first name so appropriate. Being beasts of burden, not much in Humphry or Jack's lives brings joy. Humphry has learned to see his life from the light side. Jack wrestles the darkness.

One day, trekking miles in discouraging heat, Humphry and Jack saw their destination appear on the horizon.

Humphry said, "Look, we're almost there."

"Almost there. It will take all afternoon," answered Jack.

Humphry felt compelled to speak despite the disagreement and hard feelings that would follow.

"Jack. Why do you view every challenge from the dark side?

"I'm not dark. I'm just honest. You know it will take all afternoon. Would you rather I lied or covered my feelings?"

"It's not your feelings I want to imprison," said Humphry. "I don't want lies. I just want you to look at things a new way. It's difficult to have a friend who sees the dark side of everything. It makes the work so much harder."

Jack had a hard time understanding. Practicality ruled his life.

But there's a difference between practicality and cynicism. To only see the dark side is to blacken the wondrous things of the world. When "yes, but" is our most popular phrase, we rob joy from our own lives, and the precious amount we are allotted is too rare to surrender too easily.

YAH, BUT

How do you take compliments?

If someone ventures a compliment like, "You look good today," how do you respond?

"Yah, but I feel horrible. Look at this pimple. It's like a beacon shining to the world."

A simple "thank you" would make both the giver and receiver feel a lot better.

Here's a few more examples. See if you recognize yourself:

"That show was great. Wasn't it original? Wasn't it moving?"

"Yah, it was fantastic. But did you notice the terrible way they cut from one scene to the next?"

Or:
"Great shirt."

"Yah, but by the end of the day it will be wrinkled."

Or:
"Do you want to go to the movies?"

"Yah, but we won't get a babysitter. It looks like rain. What if ...?"

HUMAN COMPLEXITIES
AREN'T BLACK
AND WHITE.
THEY'RE EVERY
SHADE OF GREY.
DON'T LET
THE DARK SIDE
CREEP INTO
THE BRIGHTNESS
OF THE DAY

Try listening to how you talk. If there are always conditions on compliments or actions, eliminate them from your conversation. Just don't add the "but." You'll find you generate a lot more enthusiasm for your endeavors. And the more you do it, the less often conditions and qualifiers will intrude into your life.

Sure, things will still go wrong, we'll still trip. The "but" may still happen, the rain may still fall. It was going to anyway. If you bathe your thoughts in light, negative events won't look nearly as oppressive as they do from the shadows. Looking from the light side, the darkness will not seem so bleak.

Like everything in this book, though, following the advice once isn't good enough. The only way to imprint the ideas is to repeat, and repeat and repeat. Sure it's hard.

BUT it is the only way.

WE AREN'T RESPONSIBLE FOR ANY OTHER CREATURE ON THIS PLANET

This is a second payoff for taking responsibility for ourselves. We shed responsibility for the lives of others. While we have a personal onus to help, guide, teach and care for others, it is easy to go too far. Many of us end up trying to run other's lives or feel responsible for the lives around us. We can help. But we aren't responsible for the paths others follow. Our responsibility ends, when we have given our best, whether our advice is heeded or ignored. Ultimately, what others do is not our responsibility.

Similarly, we can't live other's lives for them. The ring your son wears in his nose, may look painful and grotesque — to us. Just because you wouldn't adorn yourself that way, doesn't mean no one can.

Attempted suicide often can be a call for help. Be there for a troubled friend, relative or stranger. Offer advice, help. Do as much as you can. Once you've done as much as you can, you can do no more. That troubled person may take another bottle of pills and turn again to you. Call an ambulance. You can do no more.

Here's another tough one. Your teenage daughter scoffs at your fear when she travels the street at night. Warn and warn and warn. Set rules. Then let her go. She should not be a prisoner of your fear. She has the right to become her own person, with her own fears, dreams and ambitions.

Humphry reinforces the lesson. Responsibility for his own actions means that when the camel starts a job, he finishes it. Now, he could lecture another creature about determination, discipline or control, and he can show it by his own actions. But, if after all this, the other beast of burden quits, he has tried. And Humphry will still finish what he set out to do.

MAKE YOUR OWN JOURNEY

ANYTHING IN LIFE IS YOURS
IF YOU WANT IT BADLY ENOUGH

Envy is a powerful force. There are two ways to deal with it. We can complain about what others have and put ourselves down for setting our wants farther than our grasp. With this first route, the circle of envy remains unbroken. We're forced to endure it every time we think of others' possessions or successes. Or, if we decide we're not satisfied with what we have, we have to go out and get what we want.

An old newspaper article about fitness buff Jack Lalanne elaborates my second point:

> To celebrate his 70th birthday, Lalanne swam a mile with his hands and feet tied while towing 70 small boats with a person in each. The two-and-a-half-hour swim was to demonstrate Lalanne's life-long philosophy that anything is possible with the conditioning of mind and body.

Now, Jack, I'm sure, didn't get up on his 70th birthday, gather 70 people and say, "Want to go for a boat ride?"

I'm guessing Lalanne's plan went something like this.
At 60 or 65 he decided he wanted to do something spectacular for his seventh decade, something to show people who he was and what he stood for.

He probably started swimming the route. Then he tied his hands. Then his hands and feet. Once that was perfected, he started towing boats: one, then two, then three ...

On his 70th birthday, he did it all. He accomplished his goal. He had a dream, he visualized it, he planned it, and he executed it.

There's an old saying, "How do you eat an elephant?" Answer: "One bite at a time."

No job is too big, no task too great, if you take it one step at a time. Advance bit by bit and you will accomplish just about anything you want.

If you give 100 percent, you've given as much as you can. Humphry suffers jests about his appearance, that a camel is no more than a horse put together by committee. He knows he is not the best-looking, the fastest or the richest. He knows he'll always be a camel. Yet, because he is the best camel he can possibly be, he can stand with his head held high, and grin that amused, self-assured grin.

WHAT IS IT WE REALLY WANT, ANYWAY?

When I taught a section on VALUE for Ontario Real Estate courses at Humber College, it went something like this:

FOR TRUE VALUE TO BE PRESENT:

1) THERE MUST BE A NEED
If you don't feel you need the job, the relationship, the new car, the hug, etc. you will not see the value in it.

2) IT MUST HAVE UTILITY
In other words, the something must be useful to you, whether practical or aesthetic.

3) IT MUST BE RELATIVELY SCARCE
Scarcity is probably most important of the three steps that determine value.

Consider this scenario:

It is autumn and you're creating an art project that requires fall leaves. You wouldn't pay anything for the leaves because they are abundant, just a tree away. But if the same project on autumn was due in spring or winter, the scarcity of fall leaves would probably lead you to buy them to complete the project. Suddenly, the leaves would have a cash value.

Scarcity also holds true in business. There are hundreds of mediocre middle-managers. There are only few who are aggressive, caring, creative and brimming with human skills. And the same goes for personal relationships. Most of us would give just about anything to have that perfect partner who can give us everything we think we need. They are scarce.

Just think of how many acquaintances you have compared to how few close friends. Reflect on the scale of value you put on both friendships.

To have value, a thing must fulfill a need, it must be useful and it must have qualities that are relatively scarce.

And finally,

4) YOU MUST HAVE THE PURCHASING POWER
To get something of value you have to have the dollars to pay. No matter how much the need, no matter how useful the item, no matter the scarcity, if you can't or won't pay the price, you're not going to get it.

It holds true with relationships and desires. Think of your needs. It could be for a special someone perhaps, or for a thing, such as losing weight or gaining a promotion. The need may be real and you see its usefulness. It may be scarce, but if you aren't willing to pay the price — to sacrifice or compromise or do whatever is necessary — then value has not been created to your satisfaction.

That's why it is said, "Value is determined by the PERCEPTION of value."

VALUE IS THE RELATIONSHIP BETWEEN PEOPLE AND THE THINGS THEY DESIRE

When we desire something, its value is not arbitrary. When we see value, or worth, in something or someone, it must be based on personal beliefs of value, NOT the result of coercion by peer pressure, tradition or shame.

Ask yourself these questions:
- Do I really NEED this?
- Will I really USE this?
- Is this the ONLY ONE around?
- Am I willing to PAY THE PRICE to get it?

Because each of us has different needs and wants, value is a relative thing. Value is a personal commodity and we must see beyond our preconceptions and learn to respect what other people consider as valuable.

YOU HAVE NO RIGHT TO JUDGE OTHERS. NO ONE HAS THE RIGHT TO JUDGE YOU

Taking responsibility for our own actions — determining our own destiny — keeps getting more beneficial. Live by the first part of the above statement, and demand the second. Breathe a sigh of relief. Now we don't need to worry about what people think of our looks, our jobs, or positions. Now we can measure our success by our own yardstick, no one else's.

Remember the simple philosophy from the first chapter:

EVERYONE CAN DO ANYTHING
THEY WANT AS LONG AS
IT DOESN'T ADVERSELY AFFECT OTHERS

Keep that in mind. Wear green hair if you want to. Speak in rhyme if you've got the time. Just make sure that you're doing it because you want to and not to shock or please others. That will only put you back on the spiral of destruction this book wants to lead you from.

WAYS TO MANAGE YOUR PERSONAL RELATIONSHIPS

I have a few examples, drawn from my life and others around me, that illustrate the different ways we manage our personal relationship.

St. Catharines, where I've lived my whole life, is close to the U.S. border. When I was a teenager, the drinking age was 21 in Ontario and 18 in New York State. Driving "over the river," as we called it, became a weekend ritual. Regularly, I would get totally drunk. Then I'd get sick. The thing is, I did this all through my teens. I hated the taste of booze. I despised it, but I thought drinking and partying was the only way to keep my friends. Keeping them meant doing exactly what they wanted to do even if I didn't want to.

It took until my 20s before I realized I didn't have to drink alcohol if I didn't want to. That my true friends and business associates would remain a part of my life if I didn't drink. Of course, there were some who made an issue of my self-assertion. At first it bothered me but eventually I realized that these people were the ones with the problem. At the same time, though, I didn't have the right to lecture them on their drinking habits. When their drinking started to adversely affect me, I eliminated them from my social circle.

This wasn't easy. In fact, at first it was harder than keeping the status quo. But, and this is a big but, once they were eliminated I never had to deal with the feeling again. If I had avoided making a stand, I'd still be battling myself and them over each drink.

DISEASES OF THE MIND

That was one way I took responsibility for my own life.

Before I tell you how Feia did it while we were still married, I'm going to let you in on something it took me a while to discover. There's a group of people that have been put on this earth just to distress and annoy other people.

It doesn't matter how nice you are, how much you do for them or how kind you are to these people. They don't change. It's because they have a disease. The disease is called ANAL CRANIAL INVERSION. (Think about it for a moment).

Sufferers of this disease do their best to push their distorted views on others. They're argumentative and destructive. They think they're never wrong. They want their affliction to be contagious.

I hope you don't recognize any friends or relatives with these symptoms. If you do, there are rules to deal with them. First, try to bring them into society. If this fails, remove them from your life. Don't let yourself be dragged to the depths of their depression.

Okay, back to Feia (pronounced Fay).

Along with being my former wife, Feia is a special friend. When we decided to have children, Feia chose to leave her existing job to be a full-time mother and raise our two daughters.

When she found out I was gay, we knew the marriage couldn't continue and we made plans to separate. But first, Feia wanted to go back to school for retraining. She decided to seek employment in the school system, to be a Special Needs Worker. When she was younger, Feia had volunteered at a centre for the physically challenged and she never lost the attraction to helping people. The bonus was she could take the same school holidays our daughters received.

The plans were very pat, but the obstacles were great. Feia was 41. She hadn't been in a classroom for 20 years. Her marriage had disintegrated. She was dealing with the shock of discovering her husband was gay and her two children needed her more than ever.

She worried for her children and her personal and professional future — even her possible exposure to AIDS. She wondered if she could ever be truly happy again.

A lot to deal with, yes. Too much to cope with, no.

Feia enrolled in a two-year diploma course at a local college. She became a full-time student surrounded by classmates half her age. To top it off, there was a personality conflict with her supervisor, which meant everything Feia did had to be a little better than the norm. But having to work harder, to be that much better, wasn't all bad.

As time passed, Feia became more and more enthusiastic, putting more and more into her work. She realized she had what it took to be the best at what she wanted. Suddenly, she was enduring and conquering all that came before her.

Feia graduated in June of 1990 from Niagara College with a 92-point average. She made the Dean's List each semester and received the Faculty Award for the highest average in her graduating class.

As I write this book, Feia has landed a full-time job as a childcare worker. All the obstacles aren't cleared yet, but I notice a new calmness and self-confidence in Feia that I've never seen before. Now, she is not only a special friend but my advisor and comforter, my mentor and confidant.

Feia has taught me a great deal and there always will be a special love for her in my heart.

THE OTHER SIDE

Success stories, unfortunately, aren't the whole of our existence. Some people don't know how to break out:

Ms M is obviously a person unhappy with her personal relationship. She constantly tries to prove she's right. If she's challenged, she gets very irritable. Ms M has many friends but she is alienating them because of how she flies off the handle without warning. Ms M also drinks too heavily at times.

Underneath, Ms M is a very caring and giving person. But, because she can't be honest and open with herself about who she is, she suffers hours and hours of anguish.

Because she thinks everyone is judging her, she believes she can judge others, and then verbalize her judgments. I know most of her friends and family and all we want from her is for her to remember who she is, to be herself.

PAUL

I lived this next story:

Paul was magical. He was an illusionist and showman. He was about 25, good-looking and surrounded by friends. He was also very proud. From an early age he ran a very successful business that earned him a good income.

But the illusionist couldn't separate his illusion from reality. Paul thought that the only way to get and keep friends was to party and pay his friends' way. He didn't know he was liked simply because he was likable.

A problem developed. Like a lot of us who think we have to buy our friends (and I was like this for many years), Paul spent more than he made. Eventually the business collapsed under debt. And with that loss came the loss of the friendships of people who had invested in the business.

Apparently this hurt Paul deeply. But he never let it show. He regrouped and started a new business with his partner. Things went well — at first — but Paul didn't learn his lesson. Extravagant expenditures created problems. Subsequently his partner moved out.

None of us knew how hurt, lonely and unhappy Paul became. He never allowed anyone inside the illusion. We can only imagine the pain of his last days and hours. I wrote his eulogy, Paul hung himself.

QUESTIONS?

Which one of us can truly say
he understands the pain?
Which one of us can think of Paul
and not consider blame?
Who among us sitting here
can say within his heart
that he had done his very best
to play the "friendship" part?
Were there signs we didn't see?
Were cries for help unheard?
Or did we simply think that he
knew how to say the word?
Help! Please help me. I am close.
I'm closer every day
I cannot take this pain. Please help.
Please make it go away.
What do you think he must have felt
when he knew he had no voice?
To speak. To say the words.
To cry for help. The cry.
To ask for answers to his questions.
No one will know why.

Feia Korolevich
August 28, 1991

THE END OF THE ILLUSION

Are you living an illusion? Have you created a magical mystical person for your friends and family to admire? Take off the mask. Show people who really care about you who you really are. Let them see how the trick is performed. Let them in on your little secrets. Be the real you. Those who care will still be there. Those who don't weren't worthy of the illusion in the first place.

I think these stories show how important our relationship with ourselves is. Some of us have a good relationship, others do not. Many of us are somewhere in between, and still working on it.

Be patient. Keep trying. It isn't easy to overcome the years of hurt or the misconceptions we have about ourselves and others. But don't give up. And don't despair.

REMEMBER:
- You are unique. No other creature can feel the things you feel or be the type of person you can be.
- Don't judge others and they can't judge you.
- You are responsible for your own life. Don't relinquish that responsibility.
- You are not responsible for anyone else's life. Let them take their own journey.
- You can attain anything you want in life if you want it badly enough.

Keep these thoughts on the surface of your mind. Be happy. No one else will make you happy except you. Be proud. You are special and no other creature has the right to put you down.

Here are ten little words that sit on my desk. I don't know who the author is, but they're widely repeated:

IF IT IS TO BE
IT IS UP TO ME

OUR RELATIONSHIPS
WITH OTHERS

OUR RELATIONSHIPS WITH OTHERS

As I mentioned earlier, Feia and I are special friends. We've tried to maintain contact with our old friends:

In 1991, one of our friends was turning 40 and her husband planned a surprise party for her. He called me for my new address and sent an invitation addressed only to me. Both these people know I'm gay and they both knew my former boyfriend, Darius. We've even visited their home. I assumed that omitting Darius' name was an oversight so I called and asked if it would be OK to bring him. The birthday woman's mother-in-law said yes. With that, I thought no more and Darius and I made plans to attend.

Later, while talking to Feia, she asked if I was sure Darius was invited and I related the telephone call. But Feia remained concerned. She didn't have a problem attending with Darius and I, as we had been together at several functions, but she was troubled that our friends' family didn't know I was gay and would be bringing my partner.

Knowing how cavalier I am about such things, Feia decided to call and double check. The husband told Feia that the invitation did not include Darius. Needless to say, I was quite miffed, frankly upset, especially since I knew that this particular couple were not homophobic in any way. I guessed the husband was concerned how his parents and other guests would react to us being there.

Darius and I ended up staying away from the party and watched a few movies instead. A few days later the woman whose party it was called to say how upset and embarrassed she was about the situation. She said that one of the first things she noticed when she arrived was that Darius and I were absent. Of course we had been invited, she said, and added that she was very upset with her husband and couldn't understand what he had been thinking.

But don't take that the wrong way. Feia was not interfering. She just wanted to help and honestly thought she was doing what was right.

I share this example because the events are a common happening. "A" is concerned about a situation and wants to help. When "A" enters the picture, things go BOOM ...

Had my well-meaning ex-wife not called, Darius and I would have attended the party and likely there would have been no problems. When I talked to Feia later about it she said, "I've learned something today. From now on I'll stay out of your business."

There's a lesson here.

I don't think staying out of someone's business is necessarily the answer. The problem is jumping unsolicited into a situation. When we try to help someone we love, we sometimes can go a little too far. It may be difficult to do, but when I originally answered Feia's concern, she should have left it alone — no matter how hard it would have been. She raised her concern and was told it was taken care of. Her responsibility had ended.

Whether we are part of a relationship or trying to help a relationship, we have to remember that we are not responsible for someone else's life. People should be allowed to take their own journeys and make their own mistakes as they progress through life.

Depending on how we were raised, and our inborn qualities, we either become protectors or nurturers. The human traits of caring and loving are beautiful, but they're harmful as well. When something has hurt us, it is only natural to try to protect those we care about from the same circumstances.

On the receiving end, however, it becomes an outside influence. Instead of following the advice blindly, dismissing it, or becoming irritated with the intrusion, try taking the information in the manner it was meant, digest it and see how it feels. Then make your own decision based on your feelings. Decide what's best for you, not for anyone else.

FEELINGS

Have you noticed I use the word feelings a lot. It's an important word with an important meaning and I want to spend a bit of time trying to understand it.

To a lot of us — especially men — feelings are bad. A lot of us have been raised to hide or control our feelings. A lot of us have been taught to be leaders and not to show weakness. We have confused weakness with feelings. But the two don't relate. Just because a person can feel sad or happy, pained or elated does not mean that they are weak, weak in the macho concept of the word. First we must think about the distinction. Then, when we have separated the two, we can open our hearts and minds to the concept of feeling:

TO FEEL IS TO LIVE

With that said, I'm going to take you on a journey from numbness to feeling, my own journey. It's a bit erratic, but be patient. Each incident is linked by its very personal, hollowing effect on me. Each, I think, shows how we equate weakness with feeling. We all have incidents like these, moments of our lives that burn in our memory, whose fires are often controlled but never extinguished. Your circumstances may be different than mine, but our pain is the same. Only in recent years have I worked through this garbage and learned to feel, to really feel. And it's great.

CHILDHOOD

My father worked for General Motors in St. Catharines. Then, wages were poor and strikes and layoffs were common. My mother became a waitress to earn extra income. We lived in various rental properties and my parents never owned a car.

I was the oldest of four children. When I look back, I can see how my years without many material things gave me the drive I needed to be a success and an achiever. At 13, I took a job as a busboy and have worked since. When I was 16, I bought the first car in our family. My father cosigned for the loan.

This started an up and down relationship with credit. My father always borrowed his way out of problems and it taught me how easy it was to live on credit. Many times I've borrowed more than I could pay back.

I remember driving my father to a finance company when I was about 17. The loans officer requested my mother's signature on a loan application. My father said my mother was ill and took the document, saying he'd return with her signature. When we sat in my car, he forged my mother's name. Later I drove him back to pick up the money. Good lesson, right? I was told this was something my mother had already agreed to and the signature was just a formality.

Of course, I knew that wasn't true. I kept quiet though. The script I was given didn't allow me to reveal my true feelings. Only now, as I write this book, am I telling what happened that day. For almost 26 years, those feelings of betrayal have been locked up inside me.

BE A MAN ...

Another time, while walking home from school, four boys surrounded me because they thought I was after the girlfriend of one of the boys (if he only knew). The leader told me to leave her alone and ended up kicking me in the groin. I ran home and told my father. He jumped up and started after them, barreling over six fences before they got away. When dad returned he said that had he caught the boy, he would have dragged him back so I could fight him (the boy) like a man, one-on-one. One-on-one like a man!

I couldn't tell my father how I felt. I couldn't say, "Dad, I'm afraid. I don't want to fight." If my father had actually caught them, I would have had to fight. That's the way it was. At least that was my perception of the way it was.

There also were nights I lay awake listening to my parents argue. Usually both were drunk and my father had gambled most or all of his pay away. Voices were loud and ashtrays flew through the air. As the oldest, I was taught, and taught myself, to stay in control and hide my emotions and feelings, to be a pillar of strength.

THE ACHIEVER

Don't get me wrong. My childhood wasn't hell. All this, in some way, urged me to achieve. I was captain of the football team, a gold-medal oarsman, vice president of the student council, an actor in variety shows, and, most important to me at the time, a fraternity member. Yes. I was a member of the all-male, jock fraternity. It was the ultimate in status.

It made me feel important, part of the group. That fraternity jacket made me feel special.

FAMILY BREAKDOWN

During my late teens, strange things started to happen between my parents. Outside influences were at work. My mother's family is Catholic, my father's Armenian. My mother's mother died when my mother was very young and it affected mom deeply. My mother's father, a very successful businessman, was a strict taskmaster. After many misunderstandings, they finally planned to straighten things out, but before they cleared the air, her father suffered a heart attack and died. My mother lives with this, and the unresolved feelings have caused innumerable problems. It led to alcoholism, addiction to pharmaceutical drugs and several suicide attempts. Pretty messed up.

There was a time in my life when my relationship with my mother was very poor. In fact, despite living in the same city, we didn't see each other for almost three years. Now I understand some of the reasons why she is the way she is. I also understand the reasons I am the way I am. When we see each other now, we can even have a good time. In fact, I'm proud of her, now, she is trying to put her life together. What I have to remember is that her life is her journey and all I can do is help her, not take her journey for her.

MARRIAGE

I became engaged to Feia at age 20. When I brought her home to my parents' house, to share our great news and joy, my father said, "Good. Now take me to my sister's. Your mother and I are separating." Ouch.

But I was the oldest, I was supposed to do the mature and strong thing. I drove my dad to his sister's and kept all my disappointment and anger inside. My parents were separated for six months, then renewed their vows.

From time to time, I still guard my true feelings, and its a blockage in my relationships. It was only a few years ago that I was able to cry in public. In the past, if I failed at something or didn't get what my heart had been set on, I would just shrug and pretend it didn't matter or say, "Maybe next time."

How did I learn to cry in public, to show my true feelings, to be the real me?

I guess it happened when I realized I was gay, accepted it, and finally came out of the closet. It was then that I was able to be the true me, to act the way I was meant to act, to feel the way I was meant to feel. That means that if something sad enough to make me cry happens, even if it happens in public, I'll cry.

CLOSETS AREN'T JUST FOR GAYS

We're all in some sort of closet. Each one of us wears a mask, hiding our true self underneath. To show our feelings in public, we're forced to unmask ourselves, to be vulnerable to recognition.

Whatever your closet is, try to open the door and enter the world as you truly are. Then you won't have to hold back the tears. You can hug again without discomfort or guilt. You will be able to feel life the way it was meant to be felt. Remember, closets are for clothes, not people.

DON'T MISLEAD YOURSELF

Our tendency to hide our feelings or refuse to react to them does our relationships an injustice. Other people in our lives can't read minds. They can only react to what they see. So when we don't show our true feelings, we don't get a true reaction. Each time it happens, the gap in the relationship widens. At the same time, just like the boy who cried wolf, overcompensation or sensitivity to an extreme belittles the reactions and causes distrust of those very feelings we want so much to share.

What I try to do is trust my first reaction to a situation, to use that first feeling as a guide. Even still, I hold back feelings to avoid unnecessary fights or bad feelings in my relationships. This is the balance between dignity and adversely affecting others.

What we must attempt to discuss, as clearly and precisely as possible, are our true feelings with the other persons in our relationships. Never take a stance of right or wrong. Just address the problem. When you first clarify your feelings, you deal with the true issues.

In the end, it is a rare occasion that we can change the other person or alter their perception of a situation, and even if we do, the change is usually short-lived. The most we can do is try to understand how the other person feels, accept it, and then deal with our personal feelings about the situation.

A FABLE

Have you heard the fable of the frog and the scorpion? It goes something like this:

> One day, a frog is at a river when a scorpion comes along and asks the frog to take it across.
>
> The frog says, "No. If I do that, you'll sting me and I'll drown."
>
> "I wouldn't do that," the scorpion says. "I'd drown too."
>
> So the frog is convinced and as they cross the river, the scorpion stings the frog.
>
> "Why do that?" the frog asks. "Now we'll both die."
>
> "It's in my nature," answers the scorpion.

Unfortunately, this piece of fatalism rings true. Most people can't change their inherent nature. Frogs and scorpions have their human counterparts. If you let a scorpion come close, be prepared for the sting.

"I've changed," is one saying that often rings hollow. Alcoholics, who no longer drink, are still alcoholics. Violent people who no longer hit are still violent. Change is possible, but basic nature usually remains the same.

AAAH, LOVE

On a more pleasant side, let's revel in the past for a moment. Aaah, love. Remember the warmth of your first love? Imagining the rest of your life together? Finding everything you were seeking? Your lover was perfect. You offered your heart and soul to the relationship. Remember how you always looked at each other, always touched when you were together. Remember those long hours staring into each others' eyes, holding hands. Life was perfect. Nothing could ever go wrong.

If a friend or family member had the gall to point out an imperfection, you took great exception or lashed out in protective fury. But for some of you the seed of doubt was planted and ever-increasing portions of time and energy in the relationship were thrown into changing your partner into something he or she wasn't and would never be.

But let's step into our partner's shoes. The closer we are, and the more in love we are, the more defensive we get when our partner tries to remake our image into their ideal, into what will best suit them. It isn't a selfish move. They really do care about us, and they want the best.

SO WHAT IS THE MOTIVE?

Sometimes our mate is trying to renew a lost love, or recreate a parent figure or find strengths he or she are without. Maybe you are just a springboard from a bad situation.

It is possible to learn their real intentions. It is a question of understanding, of digging as deep as we can, of communicating openly. But it isn't as easy as it sounds. Paul refused to let anyone inside. I, too, was one of those people. But I recognize the fault. I was brought up with the notion that strength forbid the exhibition of weakness or emotion. If partners asked if I was OK I could only agree. I put my ex-wife through hell because my guard was always firm. And I suffered deeply.

But pain opens the door to joy. Now I know it is perfectly acceptable to reveal the whole me. It's still difficult, but opening your heart and soul to your partner lets him or her satisfy your needs and wants, your true needs and wants. Misrepresented feelings lead to misunderstandings and to arguments that eventually destroy the precious relationship.

Many reasons exist for this closeting of our feelings. Along with upbringing and the tradition of strength, fear plays a major role. We fear our partners will find we're not as perfect as they perceive and our faults will make them leave us. Yet, in most cases, the opposite is the result. Our partners will feel special and needed, closer to us. They'll want to help you as much as you would want to help them with their problems.

We don't know how or why we fall in love with certain people. All we know is we get this incredible feeling that we have to act on, regardless of how many checks we can mark on that secret list of wants we've compiled for a lover.

Remember Martin Luther King's priceless words. "A heart can only love another heart." It is most unfortunate that society or our family tries to intimidate our choice of hearts. And that brings us back to successful relationships.

ΗΛΡΡΙLУ ΕVΕR ΛFTΕR

Most of us were raised with the idea that we grow up, meet someone, fall in love and spend the remainder of our lives together in happy, wedded bliss. Hand in hand with the idea that separation or divorce is failure, a failure to ourselves, our partners, our children, our parents, our church and our society as a whole. So we feel we should stay in an unsuccessful relationship, even for the wrong reasons.

I've named this fallacy "El Toro Doo Doo", which translates as bullshit.

This book is intended to help you strengthen relations, not destroy them. It also allows for honorable exits.

The only person we can change in a relationship is ourselves. If we can't live with a certain set of circumstances, then we should seriously consider ending the relationship. That's right, end it. If you have done your best to adjust and alter your attitude and you're still bothered and confused about your relationship, then call it quits — at least in its present form.

I say each to his own journey. The most we can do is learn and understand and care. Each experience brings us closer to our own spiritualism.

Partners can go their separate ways and retain good feelings between themselves. What marks failure is blame, and blame stains and buries the wonderful memories and the reasons why we first fell in love.

NOTHING IS FOREVER

All relationships, with family, friends and loved ones, go through phases where each individual takes a different path. Sometimes these paths along the road of life never rejoin. It's hard but true. I don't believe the old adage: "You made your bed, now lie in it." Life is too short to spend your days in a relationship that doesn't work for you. That's not to give you a green light to jump in and out of relationships whenever things aren't going your way. But if you've done everything you can to understand and salvage a relationship, even taking it to counseling, and it still causes you grief or affects your health, it is time to alter it. This includes all relationships — your lover, family, friends, acquaintances and especially your working relationships.

The key to successfully ending a relationship without bitterness is to realize that there was no right side and no wrong side. Realize that no single person is to blame, that there was no fault, only that the relationship didn't work for specific reasons. By keeping curled the pointing finger of blame, you can avoid hate. As far as I'm concerned, the most powerful destroyer of life is hate.

You'd think that telling your wife you're gay is a sure way to end a relationship, but that doesn't have to be the only solution. When I unburdened my secret, Feia and I realized our marriage was over. But our relationship hadn't ended, it had simply changed. I'll never forget what Feia said the night we were discussing our next move. She said, "I don't want this thing to ruin a 20-year friendship." We had been partners and friends. No longer partners, we remained friends. We talk more now than we did when we were married.

Feia and I kept up that special feeling we have for each other, through some very tough times and even through the insistence of so-called friends who tried to destroy our new relationship. Here are a few samples of the "helpful support" we received:
- "I hope you're going to make sure he pays."
- "You gave her the house? Are you nuts?"
- "He/she may be nice now, but wait till he/she turns on you."
- "What do you mean you're still good friends? That just doesn't happen."
- "How could you do this to your children?"
- "What did your family say?"
- "How will your friends react to this?"

At the same time, there were many, many good friends, real friends, who offered help, support and understanding.

My point is this:

WE MUST ENTER, TAKE PART IN, AND END ANY RELATIONSHIP IN OUR OWN WAY WHILE BALANCING CONSIDERATION FOR OUR OWN AND OTHERS' FEELINGS

Remember, relationships don't always have to end. They can change too. In most cases, if the change is done properly it will be for the better.

A very good friend of mine, Dr. Barry Joe, a professor at Brock University, gave me a version of poem on the next page which he picked up on the Internet:

AFTER A WHILE

After a while you learn
the subtle difference between
holding a hand and chaining a soul
and you learn
that love doesn't mean leaning
and company doesn't always mean security.
And you begin to learn
that kisses aren't contracts
and presents aren't promises
and you begin to accept your defeats
with your head up and your eyes ahead
with the grace of a woman, not the grief of a child
and you learn
to build your roads on today
because tomorrow's ground is
too uncertain for plans
and futures have a way of falling down
in mid-flight.
After a while you learn
that even sunshine burns
if you get too much
so you plant your own garden
and decorate your own soul
instead of waiting for someone
to bring you flowers.
And you learn that you really can endure
you really are strong
you really do have worth
and you learn
and you learn
With every goodbye, you learn ...

© 1971 Veronica A. Shoffstall

But wait! The sorrow of saying goodbye isn't an eventuality. Consider these strategies and thoughts to help preempt unnecessary trouble in your close relationships and casual friendships.

SEPARATE YOURSELF

Imagine going to bed in the suit and tie that looked so good at the office. Imagine setting out for work in pajamas.

Ridiculous, you say. And I agree. It doesn't take a brain surgeon to realize appearances should fit the situation. Why then, do we forget to change gears for the varied relationships we jump into during a day?

We get home from work, throw the coveralls in the wash and then give our mate a hard time because of an argument we had three hours before with a coworker or a friend.

Every relationship is individual. Each stands on its own. Not only is it fair to our loved ones, but treating each relationship on its own merits brings clarity to our social interactions and to each life experience.

Again, this is one thing to say, and another to do.

The "how," in this case, is to immerse yourself in the present. Let go of the past, the hard day at the office, the nagging doubts of an earlier decision. Enjoy the moment and commit totally to the time, place and person you are with. Stop mixing people and events. It's selfish to force others to react to events and moods they know nothing of. Life experiences travel well from one situation to another, emotions do not.

FEEL FOR OTHERS

When we separate the relationships in our lives, we take a step toward respecting others. To go farther, to live as a more rounded person, we need to learn to feel for others. Empathy provides the best rule book to guide our actions.

If we learned to feel what the other person is feeling, there would be no motive to inflict pain, or hurt anyone else:

- YOU know what it is like when someone yells at you, so why yell at someone else?
- YOU know what it is like when someone cuts you off in your car, so why cut someone else off?
- YOU know the feeling that happiness brings, so why not bring happiness to others?
- YOU know the warmth a big hug gives you, so give the same feeling to others.
- YOU know how good it feels when someone helps you, so why not help more people?
- YOU basked in the glow of praise for a job well done, so why not look for situations to give praise?

Before you act, ask yourself how that action is going to make the other person feel.

BEYOND THE BOOK COVER

Tagging people with labels, slotting them into categories, can be either useful or degrading. The key element is to know which you are doing. Some of us, when labeled as a certain type — brainy, slow, overweight, passive — start to take on the characteristics of that label. Remember public school?

Each class, in whatever school, had its scapegoat, a child mercilessly picked on because of something — weight, odor, height. Those labels stick and they're painful to remove, if they're ever removed.

Even in adulthood, we do the same thing. Its aim, more often, is segregation and prejudice.

WHO "THEY" ARE

We use generic phrases like "You know what 'they' are like," or "If 'they' knew what you were doing 'they' wouldn't be able to handle it."

Who the hell are 'they'? Some monster? A blank face? Something so cruel or distorted that to identify them further would give them humanity? "They," in other words, is used as an excuse to hide true feelings, to erect barriers to the truth.

In my experience, there isn't a "they". It is a mask for the speaker to reveal his own prejudices or beliefs.

When Feia and I divorced, some friends and family called us the ex-husband or the ex-wife. The label was infuriating.

We were expected to act according to some preconceived notion of what ex's were like. Suddenly Feia and I didn't exist, didn't have a choice in how to relate after divorce. We took the choice back, though, and remain on excellent terms.

Labels can be effective but I've found that if we stop taking class, rank, category, type, so seriously, we will be able to get to know and understand people. The best approach to people is on an individual basis. Find something deeper than race, color, creed, religion, job position. Accord each the dignity you demand. A person who cleans rooms for a living shouldn't be treated with any less respect than the owner of a hotel.

It is appropriate to like or dislike an individual, but how can justification be found to hate or dislike a whole group of people simply because they are black, Asian, old, young, lesbian, gay, Jewish, Muslim, Christian or even ex-husband or ex-wife?

Let's keep up with evolution.

The prejudices and customs of yesteryear may not be appropriate today. The patterns are constantly changing.

OUTSIDE INFLUENCES

Peer pressure is not just a childhood phenomenon. Adults and senior citizens can also feel this external pressure, and this social force can affect relationships in both positive and negative manners.

Because of a deep need to be loved and accepted by our friends and associates, we'll do almost anything to fit in, to be part of the "group."

In almost all groups there are leaders and followers. And whether they're good or bad leaders depends on the type of group. I simply mean some of the leaders of these "in groups" are very insecure. That is why they must control the people and circumstances around them. As long as they can use peer pressure to control the group, they'll do as they wish. If we are ever to alter the way these groups are managed, we must make it socially unacceptable to do certain acts or say certain things.

Years ago it was acceptable to use the terms "nigger" or "coon". Now it isn't. Yet it is still acceptable to call homosexuals "fags" or "queers." Hopefully someday it will not. There's been a change of attitude toward women too. Once considered inferior, emotional or fragile, these labels now are unacceptable. But still, there exist areas where peer pressure allows men to revert back to their primitive states, to cloak themselves in a Neanderthal attitude. It may be the core of their personality showing, or they may be humoring others in order to "get the business" or join the old boy's club.

How can we alter this social behavior? And is it our right, or even our task, to do so?

Let's go back to my basic philosophy:

WE SHOULD BE ABLE TO DO ANYTHING WE WANT AS LONG AS WE DO NOT ADVERSELY AFFECT ANYONE OR ANYTHING ELSE

We usually get a feeling, a red flag, when we do something that contradicts the behavioral code that says "Treat others the way we want to be treated." But in some cases, peer pressure is so intense that we ignore the warning signals and go along with "the group," but that awful feeling, that knot in the pit of our stomach, returns and says "Hey, jerk, you screwed up."

Then it is too late. The damage is done. All we can hope is that no one was injured permanently.

With our freedom to do what we want without hurting others, I suggest that it is our right, even our duty, to stop injustice, to help our neighbor, to stand up for what we believe, to make this planet better for all its inhabitants.

The next time your stomach knots, or the hairs on the back of your neck turn to bristles STOP! GET OUT! DON'T PARTICIPATE! Group acceptance isn't worth personal anguish.

THE "IN" CROWD

Humphry tells this story of his friend Jack. Early in their lives, when the desert demanded little, the two were playing. A group of other pack animals approached them and announced they were forming a new club. It was to be the "IN" crowd. Admission was stiff. To show you were worthy, you had to do two things — steal dates from the supply tent and wander two miles from camp.

Both Humphry and Jack wanted to belong. To be "IN" was strong enough reason, but they were also told that if they didn't join they would be shunned and called the most worthless of beasts for their cowardice.

Both knew the demands were wrong. Humphry stuck by his code and said no. Dignity and his disavowal of destruction, he decided, meant keeping his responsibility to his parents and society. If the other creatures couldn't respect his decision, it was their loss. He would find new companions.

Jack, however, wanted to be "IN" too badly. He couldn't stand to be teased so he did as they asked even though guilt set in immediately.

Needless to say, Jack was caught. For taking the dates he went hungry. For breaking camp, he was shunned and forced to trail the caravan for weeks.

Because of what Jack thought he had to do, whether it was peer pressure or his upbringing, Jack felt he had only one choice.

But we all do have a choice. We set our own agenda. The control of our lives is ours. To the people who laugh and ridicule us, or push us out of the group, I say: "You are diseased. Keep your distance because I couldn't stand to catch Anal Cranial Inversion."

As Humphry would say:

"DON'T LET ANYONE YANK YOUR CHAIN"

Go through life with dignity. Dignity is worth much more than buying another day's acceptance. I see the abandonment of self-esteem constantly. I've done it myself, and it's not fun.

BE THE PERSON YOU WERE MEANT TO BE NOT WHO OTHERS WANT YOU TO BE

When friends, family or others try to influence your actions or thoughts, they are generally trying to help because of a concern for your welfare. A small percentage are plainly jealous and feel inferior because of their own circumstances. So attempt to understand the motivation and use your conclusions to take appropriate action.

Listen and thank all advisors. Then do what feels right for you.

EMOTION IS NOT A WEAKNESS

Trust your feelings. Act on what your gut tells you. Investigate why you feel what you feel. Ask yourself: "Why do I feel this way about this situation?"

When we truly understand our feelings and their origins, we can solve almost any problem, and solve it in a manner best for us and the people around us.

STATUS

Status is a part of our ego that can override common sense. We spend so much time building status that we should make sure its foundation is sound. Enhance your status with what you want, not what others selfishly demand of us for their personal use.

I used to think my worth was measured by my possessions; by what new car I drove, to which golf club I belonged, by my job title, by the labels adorning my clothes. This is all OK, as long as these symbols of status are for our own benefit, not what is expected.

I travel business class, not for the status, but because I arrive at my destination better rested and in shape to do a superior job. Don't confuse personal wants and comfort with status. If, for example, a friendship is judged by the neighborhood you live in, then consider the basis of the friendship.

BLAME

We tend to blame others for disagreements or failures on our part, but there really is no such thing as right or wrong. Actually it is only our opinion about how certain situations should have been handled. I'm not talking about crimes like murder or rape or robbery, I'm talking about the everyday quirks and habits we have that can drive our friends and partners around the bend. Troy, my partner, finds it easy to drop things or misplace items after he's finished using them. I'm a neat freak and replace them immediately, everything has its place. Neither of us is wrong. Through open communication and understanding, we arrive at solutions that enables us to live together in relative comfort and peace.

Too often we think our way is the only way. The old ultimatum, if you aren't with me, you're against me is only a debating technique. We may find that to keep healthy our primary relationship, which is our relationship with ourselves, our relationship with our partner or friend must change or end. In our final conclusion, remember that the other person isn't wrong, he or she is only different.

It would be an easier planet, a better planet if people realized that everyone is different; that everyone likes and believes different things. We must stop seeing right and wrong and learn to accept differences. Live and let live. If you aren't adversely affected by the appearance or actions of another, then it isn't your concern unless it affects others or the planet. Then you should be concerned, and even act in some cases.

TAKING FOR GRANTED

I left the most important until last. How many times have you heard these words (or were the person who said them):
- "She knows I love her. I don't need to say it."
- "He can wait. I just have to finish this last report."
- "Now that you're gone, I wish I had said, 'I love you' more."
- "Don't worry about her. Work comes first."
- "Oh, he'll never leave me. He loves me too much."
- "No. I don't have to call home. They trust me."

Sound familiar. It's true that you never know how good something is until it is gone. Why is it that the more we get to know someone, the less we do to show we care? We hold more doors open for strangers than we do for the persons we care about.

When was the last time you:
- Brought home flowers or wine.
- Called just to say, "I love you."
- Gave your partner a back rub.
- Sent a funny card.
- Gave a hug when it wasn't asked for.
- Brought home something for THEM when you went to the store for YOU.
- Stopped just to look at them and smile.
- Said "no" to your personal or business acquaintances to spend time with the people you love.

It doesn't matter whether you are mother and father, brother and sister or lover and partner. It is extremely important to let those special people in your life know they aren't taken for granted, that you need and love them. Don't forget to be spontaneous. We may grow up, but we can still take off our shoes and jump into a big mud puddle.

BE THE PERSON YOU WERE MEANT TO BE,
AND ALLOW ALL OTHERS TO BE
WHO THEY WERE MEANT TO BE

THE LITTLE PEOPLE

Remember what it was like to discover hair growing under your armpits? Remember the awkwardness of school dances, of first dates? Remember the frustration of never getting your way, of how slow time passed when you were waiting?

Childhood was long ago, hard to live through and very comfortable to forget. That's the mistake. Our adult feelings cloud or rule many issues, so when we deal with children we can't forget what it was like to grow up.

Remember:
- "Ma. Can I do it, please? Everyone else is."
- "My feet are too big."
- "My nose is too big."
- "I don't have the right clothes."
- "I'm too fat."
- "I hate them and never want to see them again."
- "You don't trust me."
- "Why don't you just leave me alone?"
- "It's not fair."
- "You don't understand."
- "Please. Can I go? Come on. Let me go."

I bet you could add hundreds more to this list.

Children are the most misunderstood group of PEOPLE. Some adults don't even consider them people. This has nothing to do with race, religion, country or economic status. It breaks all barriers and reaches into families in cities, towns and villages all over the world. Remember the song: "What's the Matter with Kids Today?" Maybe it should be "What's the Matter with Adults Today?"

Here's a case in point:

CHILD: I don't want to be a doctor. I'd like to be a teacher.

PARENT: You've never let us down before. We've always wanted a doctor in the family. We want you to have all the advantages we did without.

And another:

CHILD: But I'm in love. And besides, colour shouldn't even enter into the discussion.

PARENT: We don't care. They're just not our type of people. It won't work.

And another:

CHILD: Why can't I go? It will be well-supervised and I know it will be a good experience for me.

PARENT: Because you are too young. I would never even have thought of doing such a thing at your age.

And another that hits a little closer to home:

CHILD: I'm gay, mom and dad. Try to understand. I'll answer any questions you have.

PARENT: How could you do this to us? How
            could you possibly do this to your
            family?

DOING IT TO US

When a child does something, they're not doing it to their parents. It affects us, certainly, but whatever has happened deserves a second look. The child may be going through something. It could be important for the future to understand what it is, and perhaps even support them.

Remember that ring adorning our child's nose? Maybe it was his or her way of making a mark to show a difference. Perhaps it was a mark for acceptance. Perhaps he or she just liked and wanted it for themselves and it was a spur of the moment decision.

UNCONDITIONAL LOVE

We always want the best for our children, but by applying outdated techniques of child rearing we can destroy faster than we can build. We are only echoing what we were taught as we grew up. If we were taught that a woman is chattel (a man's property), we'll probably teach that to our children both by how we speak and how we act. If we were poor, there is a good chance we'll want our children to be rich and end up creating over achievers. If we were given all we wanted there is a good possibility we will allow our children to grow up getting anything they ask for (except love in a lot of cases).

In one sentence I can tell everything a child wants:

JUST LIKE US, OUR CHILDREN WANT TO FEEL NEEDED, TO BE LOVED UNCONDITIONALLY AND TO BE VALIDATED

As Feia and I were slowly separating, our youngest daughter, Brodie, experienced personality changes. As president of the Ontario Real Estate Association, and traveling with my sales training workshop, I was often away from home. Feia was in school full-time getting her diploma and Jordin, my older daughter, entered junior high school. Brodie was cast adrift. She was used to having her big sister at the same school, her mother at home after school and her father to kiss her good night. Her life was turned upside down; she was alone and fending for herself. Brodie became moody and abusive. She started to challenge authority. At first Feia and I wondered what hit our little girl. Then it hit us. She felt confused and lonely. Brodie needed attention. She needed to feel important. She needed to feel wanted. She needed to be validated.

Once we started to focus our attention on Brodie she returned to being the Brodie we knew and loved. Well, not quite. She grew from the experience. She actually became a more sensitive and caring person. Still, it shouldn't have been up to Brodie to attract our attention.

WE ARE THE ONES THAT HAVE TO WATCH HOW WE TREAT THOSE WHOM WE REALLY CARE ABOUT

Brodie, from time to time, still gets inadvertently left out. And sometimes we take her for granted because she's the youngest. The whole experience did give her a bit of an image problem but with constant praise and lots of love and attention she is starting to bloom as the person she was meant to be.

We as parents seem to jump from ignoring our children to over-reaction and over-protection. Balance is important in our relationships. We should trust the fact that our children, with strong guidance, love and understanding, will usually make the decision that is right for them (not us). Even if the decision proves to be incorrect, the child must know they can come home and find that unconditional love waiting inside the door.

DISTRUST IS ONE OF THE BIGGEST CONTRIBUTORS TO THE CREATION OF A DYSFUNCTIONAL RELATIONSHIP WITH A CHILD

I know this single mother who has a daughter who just turned 15. I'll call the daughter J.T. She was friends with a 17-year-old boy. The rule of the house was that J.T. could have no boys over unless her mother was home. One evening J.T. arranged for this boy to visit between 8 and 9 p.m. Suddenly, her mother remembered a function she had to attend. Because it left J.T. alone, her friend was not allowed to come over.

My phone rang. It was J.T. She said it wasn't fair that her mom wouldn't let her friend come over. She felt her mother didn't trust her. She asked me to call her mother.

I told J.T. that it was not right for me to interfere with the rules of her house. I went on to tell her to use her head and explain her point of view to her mother. Luckily, J.T.'s mother has always kept the philosophy that if an argument was logical and sensible, she'd agree with it.

J.T.'s conversation went something like this:

"Mom, I think what you're doing isn't fair. You always say I'm too young to do certain things. You say that when I'm 18 I can do what I want. You don't trust me to do the right thing now!"

Her mother then said it wasn't J.T. she didn't trust, but her friend.

"You're trying to keep me inside this bubble until I turn 18," J.T. said. "And then you'll burst the bubble and let me loose. If I'm not allowed to experience life and make some mistakes, can you imagine what could happen to me when I finally get out there? Trust me to handle this situation. We will only be alone for one hour, and I can assure you that I know how to handle myself."

"I know right from wrong. You have to let the rope out bit by bit. Please, mom, trust me to make the right decision."

Yes, I know it sounds too perfect. You're saying to yourself that a 15-year-old isn't that smart, that she's too irresponsible to think that way.

It's been a while since the incident and they may not be the exact words, but the substance of the conversation is unaltered.

And J.T.'s maturity enhances my point. We, as adults, need to look at children as individuals, not as statistics or gender or labels.

EACH CHILD IS UNIQUE.
EACH CHILD IS AN INDIVIDUAL.
EACH CHILD HAS THEIR OWN MATURITY.
EACH CHILD MUST BE TREATED ACCORDINGLY.

And, yes, J.T. had her friend over and all went well.

The old answer: "Because I'm your parent, that's why!" doesn't work anymore. Respect and authority are earned. Sure, there will be times when you and your child agree to disagree. That's OK. But do your best to feel what your child is feeling and try to remember what it was like when you were growing up. You can protect your child without destroying their self esteem. These guides below are for dealing with children, but they can also work in just about all relationships.

For those of you who still have parents living, I have a another piece of advice. Try to remember parents have the same feelings you do. They, too, want to be needed, loved and respected. They deserve the same considerations you expect from them. The fact that different generations aged with different rules and concepts of acceptability makes some of this relating very taxing. But try to be patient. Share your insights, your hopes and dreams. In most cases your parents' love will shine through.

We weren't born with a set of directions. Our parents didn't take a course called Parenting 101. They did what they thought was right, and made decisions based on their own upbringing.

Child/parent and parent/child relationships can be most rewarding and fulfilling as long as we remember the basic HUMAN SKILLS passed down from century to century. Revisit and rediscover these vital skills:

TRY TO FEEL WHAT THEY FEEL.
DO NOT PRE-JUDGE.
YOU'VE LIVED YOUR LIFE,
LET THEM LIVE THEIRS.
ENCOURAGE, DON'T DISCOURAGE.
CRITICIZE THE DEED,
NOT THE PERSON.
LET THEM BE THE PERSON THEY
WERE MEANT TO BE.
MAKE JUST AND FAIR RULES.
TREAT THEM WITH RESPECT.
TRUST THEM.
LOVE UNCONDITIONALLY.
BE THEIR FRIEND
NOT THEIR MASTER.
PRAISE THEM WHEN THEY TRY.
HUG THEM WHEN THEY
DON'T NEED IT.
HOLD THEM WHEN THEY
DO NEED IT.

CORPORATE RELATIONSHIPS

CORPORATE RELATIONSHIPS

Most of us spend at least 40 hours a week at work. That's a lot of time — especially if it is an unpleasant experience filled with problems and anxiety. We may know we're miserable and unhappy, perhaps realize how it affects other aspects of our lives and even concede that our personal relationships shouldn't be embroiled in our working woes.

But the fact that we spend so much time at work makes it all the more important that we learn how to enjoy it, or at the very least, tolerate those 40 hours without damaging the other facets of our lives.

But it's not as easy as snapping our fingers.

Perhaps we don't even know why or how we sank into our current position. But we easily say, "we're stuck, we're trapped." For some reason — resistance to upsetting the status quo — it is comforting to think there's no way to get ourselves out. Families, bills, obligations: these are not light considerations.

But don't look to me or Humphry for support. The tenet of this book hasn't changed:

ANYONE CAN DO ANYTHING THEY WANT
IF THEY WANT IT BADLY ENOUGH

You can control your day. You can make the work week happy and productive. Attitude is what it takes. Confucius put it simply: "A person who finds the job they love will never have to work a day in their lives."

Only the few who love their job or career truly understand this statement. Those who don't, keep reading.

Personal and professional relationships have much in common. Most work problems aren't really caused by the actual job if the job is the least bit challenging. The bulk of job frustration, anxiety, fretting, disillusionment, is caused by the people we work with and how we work with them.

Although I generally disagree with labels, I've drawn up a list of the types of people we come in contact with during the working day. This is one of those times "categorizing" problem colleagues will give a step toward dealing with them. And recognizing the types might bring a little humor to the workplace. It might also free up some time to worry about more important things, the reason you're working in the first place.

Relationships at work surround you in a triangle: At the top, is THE BOSS. This person can be the type for whom you would cut your wrists, or the type whose wrists you'd like to cut. On one angle is THE CO-WORKER. By the very nature of the word, you and the co-worker stand side by side. To work with them smarter, not harder, understanding what makes them tick is a must. On the other angle is THE CUSTOMER. These are the people who buy our goods and services. Some of us may never see THE CUSTOMER, but we must all know they exist and that without them we would have no job. Most important — whether our job is in manufacturing, marketing, accounting or selling — uppermost in our mind should be that the first and foremost person to serve in your organization is THE CUSTOMER.

You're in the center of this person-heavy triangle. You're surrounded by the pulls and friction of all their needs and demands, but you can exercise a measure of control on the strains of your work day. Power plays aren't what I'm talking about. It's attitude. Yours.

If we generalize a little, we'll realize that most people in their role as, THE BOSS, THE CO-WORKER, THE CUSTOMER and YOU, fit common personality types. I've named them and given a few suggestions about how to deal with them. The most important thing to know, however, is that you can't change them. The best you can hope for is to smooth out as many wrinkles at your end as possible. That will at least make the ride a little more comfortable.

First off, remember the disease I discussed earlier, that "anal cranial inversion" that can only be dealt with by avoidance. Avoid this dangerous, sad person, whatever role he or she happens to play. If you're cornered, smile, nod agreeably, and think of a sunny Saturday in your backyard without them.

THE WORKAHOLIC

The workaholic eats, plays, dreams and totally lives work. Time off is foreign and scary. The workaholic usually has to keep in touch with some aspect of work twenty four hours a day and seven days a week. When or if they ever take a holiday, they pack their work in their suitcase too. These people — and here's where the friction may arise — don't understand why anyone would want a life outside of work.

These are demanding people. You must try to fulfill their demands, as many of them as you possibly can without sacrificing your own privacy or leisure time. That means being available when they need you. It means increasing your workload if it's possible. It means being just as sharp and enthusiastic at 5 p.m. as you were at 9 a.m.

If all else fails, look for another job. You don't need the grief.

If YOU are the workaholic, try to lighten up a bit. The company will get along without you for an hour, a day or even (yes, I know it sounds unbelievable) a week!

At work, remember that not everyone has the same commitment to the job that you do. It isn't disloyalty. It's perspective. And it's also self-protective. Most people need time away from work to recharge their motivation. If you can allow them to recharge without calling them at home, they will be able to do a better job when they get to work.

THE PERFECTIONIST

Like the workaholic, the perfectionist can be a Royal Pain. It must be better than perfect. It must be righter than right. And then there is always something to criticize before praise.

To deal with the perfectionist, be prepared. Remember to double check everything you do. Your content must be unquestionable and your presentation flawless. If you must win over the perfectionist to a point of view, make sure your gun is loaded. That means to make sure you're armed with all the facts and you've covered all the angles. Expect criticism and be ready to highlight the positive. This can be daunting, but take confidence in the array of facts you have amassed.

To the perfectionist: Lighten up. Your drive for the absolute may worsen the finished product. Not everyone is as detailed as you. The journey through life is a series of achievements and a series of lessons. No one is perfect, not even you. The earth won't grind to a halt, as long as imperfections teach a lesson.

THE WORRIER

An obvious trait of the worrier is their insecurity, their sizable insecurity. They want to know if everything is OK, if everything is all right, if their job performance is good. They want to know again and again.

Perhaps you recognize the worrier from somewhere in middle management (uncertainty isn't the best vehicle to leadership). These people always double check arrangements, documents, plans. They're afraid of failing and can pester you with the questions: "Are you sure? Are you really sure?"

Feed this insecurity without condescension. If you're sure, be firm. If not, explain your concerns. The worrier desperately wants to know. They want reassurance or a chance to fix weak points, nothing else. No matter how firm you are, it's unlikely the worrier will wind up assured but at least he or she won't go away miffed as well. And there's one more point. Don't surprise the worrier. This frightens them a great deal. It will be as if you have broken through their security system.

Customers can be worriers too. They ask the same questions, but their determination of trust is mixed with their desire for reassurance. They're afraid their choice was wrong and they misread your character. So, if they made the right decision, tell them. And tell them why. If you can offer something better, do it. That one exchange may hold a customer for life. If you are a worrier, look back to the advice for perfectionists. Mistakes are part of life. Just tell yourself you've learned a lesson and it won't happen again.

THE "JUST-GET-BY" TYPES

These people have a bland, selfish approach to life and are most commonly found as a co-worker. They sacrifice achievement to remove stress, they make little effort and don't expect to advance. The "just-get-by" philosophy is: If I pass, I'm OK." They're also procrastinators, workers who wait until the last minute before starting a project and then do just enough to make the grade.

Do not expect to motivate someone who wants to just get by. They won't work faster or harder. They do want to pass, however, so they will not usually let you down. The finished product may not be as perfect as you would want, or as detailed, but it will be complete and it will pass inspection.

When dealing with these types, remind them of deadlines but don't waste your breath encouraging an exemplary job. Give them firmly established rules, certainly, but the "just-get-by" character has no motivation to do better. If they've been reminded, it is no longer your concern. If they fail (although unlikely), they fail on their own. Your responsibility is not for their well-being.

Try to avoid projects that bring you both together. Collaboration will be unbalanced, but don't use their attitude as a stepping stone for your gain. Stand on your own. Try a tact that offers efficiency through individual work, for example.

If collaboration is unavoidable, be prepared for sluggishness from your team member. Your control is limited. But look out for yourself. Ensure your work is complete and the best you can do. It will do two things. First, if your work shines, it ups the ante on their "just-get-by" approach. In other words, they have to work harder to pass inspection; their work can't pale beside yours. Second, their lackadaisical attitude may not be recognized the first time or the second. It may never be recognized, but your work will.

If you're the type to just-get-by, here's a word of warning: Your attitude is your own. Each of us is different, but remember, one slip in your performance, even a small one, is enough to turn that "pass" into a "fail."

THE COMPLAINER

The complainer has had a brush with Anal Cranial Inversion. Nothing Is right! Every circumstance, every person, carries something inherently wrong or misplaced.

This can be dangerous. Complainers, fighting against the world, have a tendency to stir the pot. They trust no one; their eyes see into the "Dark Side." Life is one headache after another. If the complainer won $1 million dollars, the complaints wouldn't stop.

Guard yourself when in contact with the complainer.

If they are in a superior position, be wary of their complaints and criticisms. No matter how devastatingly personal their attack may be, you remain faceless to them, a foil for their vitriol. A mistake or error (true or not) is only an invitation to attack, not the reason. Their aim is deeper, more pointed; their target is your self-confidence. The complainer, to greater or lesser degrees, wants to foster self-doubt. By doing so, the complainer's position is strengthened. Their erosion of your self-confidence is not based in truth but in positioning, in power wielding. Of course, on the face of it, an employee can't brush off the complaint of a superior. Ignoring them is dangerous. Internally, however, steel yourself to the poisonous arrows. It's a tall order, but at least know where the attack is coming from.

If your complainer is a co-worker or a customer, the same advice holds true, but, since the contact is more informal, continuous complaints can slowly erode your positive outlook. Don't let them influence your thinking. Also, don't expect to make the complainer happy about anything. It's not their nature.

Complainers are not to be ignored. This can be dangerous. They may work harder to drag you down, but there are times when it is necessary to disassociate yourself from them, whether they are a customer, co-worker or boss. Try to be as subtle as possible.

Life, as I've said numerous times, is a series of choices. You can choose a positive or negative outlook. The "Light Side" is warm and inviting; the "Dark Side" is cold and unforgiving.

It's not easy to admit you are a complainer. Some people don't even know they fit the type. Look hard at yourself. Are you being realistic or are you complaining? Take off your mask. Dare to stare into the Light Side.

THE HELPER

Generous is the best word to describe the helper. They aren't looking for pay backs or favors or perks. They want and need a sense of belonging, the comfort of fellowship. They're working very hard to keep the peace, to make the road as smooth as possible.

When you work with a helper, recognize that this is what they want. The help offered is genuine and without malice or ulterior motives. In return, be generous with your praise and thanks for their good deeds. Helpers are easy to take advantage of. Resist. The well of helpfulness is not infinite. The helper can be a good and loyal friend. They want kindness and respect.

If you are a helper, don't change. The world needs your capacity for giving. Don't help if you don't want to. That is a sure feeling you're being used. Help those who really need and deserve it.

THE BROWNER, OR, ASS-KISSER

A not-so-subtle difference exists between the helper and the ass-kisser. The browner only helps (or pretends to help) those who can help back. Their motivation is career advancement and they'll do almost anything to get it. Loyalty is a fickle ingredient in their psyche. If you aren't in a position to advance their goals, and especially if you might be in their way, expect disloyalty. The helpers and the worriers of the working world are easy prey to the browners.

If you recognize the ass-kisser at a desk next to yours, be cautious of your relationship. It isn't a relationship. It's a cease fire until a suspected weakness is exposed. Do not confide in the browner, it is a tough lesson to learn. Allow them the amount of rope they need to hang themselves.

I know the feeling of watching a browner at work. It is infuriating and transparent, at least to you. Suppress any bright ideas you have, however, of trapping the browner at his own game. It's not hard to feed bait to the starving, but a cornered person can be both dangerous and devious. Here's a second thought. Consider that your boss might like his ass being kissed. Some people do. They also don't want to admit that it strokes their ego. But don't start browning yourself. You don't have the experience — or the shallowness.

A good rule of thumb is to stand on your own two feet. Rely on your own merits for advancement. If they're not recognized, you're not wanted. Look for new employment; a place where your talents will be recognized and cultivated. Tell the potential employer that in your interview.

What advice can I give the browner? It's obvious I don't like the type and don't hold much hope for change. Let me say this: Careers come and go.

SELF-RESPECT IS THE FOUNDATION OF HAPPINESS

My personality profiles, obviously, aren't technical or scientific. They're my own opinions based on my observations and life experiences. I think, however, I've put into words what we all know in our minds.

OFFICE POLITICS

I've left one other corporate component until now: office politics. They're part of any large office, perhaps a welcome addition or a dreaded side effect to your job. I tend to feel they're the latter. Office politics, a favorite with some of the personalities I mentioned earlier, are usually about personal gain, not the betterment of the firm.

The difficult thing is to figure out which is which.

A key question to ask yourself is: "Why am I being told these things and why should I get involved?"

Most often such intrigue is all about personal gain, cloaked under concern for the firm. Personal benefit is the temptation to get involved but short term gains could bring long term losses.

So what should you do about office politics, you ask? In short, stay as far away as you can. Don't get involved.

Realistically, the problem is a little more complicated:

If you must be involved — perhaps because office moral is bad and this is a good way to help — work from a position of altruism. Avarice is a beast with a never-ending hunger. Only a few types can profit on the backs of others without remorse.

Consider your office relationships, as well. Being known as Minister of Back Stabbing is not the reputation you want. In office politics, the back bencher has a more comfortable seat.

Again, relationships are the thread of our social network, whether in the workplace or outside of the job. We can't expect others to change. We must rely on ourselves to shift and move in a way that best suits ourselves. How we treat people determines how they will treat us. Work can be a positive experience or a negative one. It depends on attitude and how we approach the tasks of the day.

Remember, Confucius says:

> "IF A PERSON FINDS A JOB
> THEY LOVE, THEY NEVER HAVE
> TO WORK A DAY IN THEIR LIVES."

Whatever your job or career, resolve to be the best worker you can be. All jobs are important. Streets need to be cleaned. Companies must have presidents. If you don't like your work, especially if it isn't challenging enough, CHANGE IT. If change is impossible, be the best you can be.

CUSTOMER RELATIONS

Personal frustrations shouldn't be taken out on customers. It doesn't matter what happened before or after you served, you have no right to inflict your problems on the customer. The advice holds true in the reverse. No customer has the right to be nasty to someone he or she has just met.

Back in August of 1988, my Auntie Edna died. She was my father's sister and my favorite relative. She helped my career as well. From her prodding, I entered real estate in 1973. That led to a high-profile position with the real estate association. which led to a speaking career and this book. I owe her much for her support and confidence.

After her death, a portion of Auntie Edna's eulogy fell to me. It was one of the most difficult speeches I've ever had to give. It was emotional and draining. That night I had to speed to Toronto to be Master of Ceremonies at a comedy roast. I couldn't cancel. I couldn't say, "Sorry, I can't be funny today." My job was to give the best show I could possibly give, to commit 100 percent. No one in the audience cared what happened to me earlier that day or what would happen after I left the roast. They paid their money and wanted the best. AND THAT IS WHAT THEY GOT!

Walt Disney said:

> ## "DO WHAT YOU DO SO WELL
> ## THAT PEOPLE WILL WANT TO COME BACK
> ## AND SEE YOU DO IT AGAIN
> ## AND THEY WILL TELL OTHERS
> ## WHAT IT IS YOU DO."

It's a simple way to succeed. Approach customers as if they will be customers for life, not a single sale. Build a relationship with the buyer, a relationship that will last. It means being fair. It means not selling them something they don't want or need. It means not tricking them into a deal. It means offering 100 percent of your attention.

The reason most customers stop dealing with a company is because of an ATTITUDE OF INDIFFERENCE on the part of the server. Earlier, I mentioned this concept of taking people for granted and it holds true for customer relations. We must look after the customers who are already giving us business. If a customer leaves happy and stays happy, you can expect them to recommend you to others. Most of us can influence at least five people to take action on our recommendation. So, if you have 100 satisfied customers, you have a potential for 500 new customers and it won't cost you a cent in advertising.

Here's a list of ways to give and get good customer service (and improve the relationships with the people you deal with on a regular basis):

HOW TO GIVE:
- Remember your customers by name and use their names as often as possible.

- Remember your customers special needs and quirks.
- Don't put together a deal just for the sake of the deal.
- Remember, the customer comes first.
- Call your customers with something that will interest them.
- Leave your personal problems at home.
- Don't bad mouth the company, other competitors or fellow employees in front of customers.
- Be honest about your service and product.

HOW TO GET:
- If the server has a name tag, use it.
- Be patient. If you are in a hurry or need something special mention it at the outset.
- If something is wrong, mention it in a responsible manner.
- Do not yell or scream and degrade the staff.
- Don't bring your problems into the transaction.
- Be courteous and show respect.
- Compliment for a job well done.

Like all relationships, customer relations follows well-beaten paths. Decide for yourself if the path is smooth or rocky.

OUR SPIRITUAL RELATIONSHIP

OUR SPIRITUAL RELATIONSHIP

Inner self. Balance. Centering. Synchronicity. Oneness with the planet.

These concepts take us on a journey to the center of our soul. Our spiritual relationship is the final spoke in the wheel of life that helps attain the balance necessary to keep us on the right track, a track that only "our" footsteps fit. It is a spiritual relationship, first and foremost with ourselves.

I will state again that although some of my ideas have been shared by many before me, the sum total that follows is Ted Mouradian's outlook, my way of conducting my life. My hope is that it will be of some assistance to you.

I don't intend to have you abandon your beliefs or to induce you to join "my club." My goal is to have you examine your belief systems and see if they are right for you, for the people you love and for the people who love you.

My beliefs are based on the concepts of free choice, unconditional love, understanding and accepting the differences in others and the golden rule of doing unto others as you would have them do unto you. If any of these strike a sour note with you, I would suggest, implore rather, that you examine your beliefs carefully.

FREE CHOICE

We all have free choice. We have a choice of getting up in the morning or staying in bed. We have a choice whether to laugh or frown. We have a choice to work or not. We have a choice to do many of the things thrust upon us each day.

I hear the qualifications. A five-year-old did not have the choice of being sexually assaulted by a parent. A terrorist does not ask before they kill. True.

What I'm talking about is that most of us do have a choice once we are given the information of the choice.

I get disturbed from time to time when people tell me, "Oh, wow, Ted. Are you ever lucky to do what you do. Are you ever lucky to be where you are. Look at me. I'm just a factory worker and I can't get out."

I disagree entirely. We can choose to live the life we were meant to live. We can choose to be the person we were meant to be.

Our biggest problem is that we always wish we could be someone else. We're not satisfied with who we are.

The 18th-century writer Baron de Montesquieu wrote:

"IF ONLY WE WANTED TO BE HAPPY,
IT WOULD BE EASY; BUT WE WANT TO BE HAPPIER
THAN OTHER PEOPLE, WHICH IS DIFFICULT,
SINCE WE THINK THEM HAPPIER THAN THEY ARE."

From time to time, people say how sorry they are to drag me somewhere, or to have called me. It's always followed by, "But thanks for coming out to help me." I say, "Don't be sorry."

Years ago, I decided to separate duty and choice. It makes life a whole lot easier if you choose to be somewhere, rather than going because it is a duty. So, if I am with someone, or I go somewhere, it is because I chose to be there.

One day, Humphry's mother asked him to get some straw for the family. He was upset. He didn't want to go. But he felt he had to. It was his duty.

As he walked, he kept getting more and more upset. Then he thought that if he brought back two bales of straw, his mother would be surprised. This made quite a difference in how he looked at the task.

One bale was Humphry's duty, two bales his joy.

If we were creatures who worked strictly on instinct, the idea of choice would be unnecessary. But we humans must choose, and choose often. We can choose what is good for us or what is not.

Seeking balance, becoming one with the self, starts with making choices that are good for us. It grows by making choices that are good for the people who love us. It blossoms by making choices that are good for the people we love.

So, be happy. Choose to be the best person you can be.

Love all things, all creatures, all persons. Choose peace, not violence. Choose tolerance, not hate. Choose truth over deceit. Live the life you were meant to live.

UNCONDITIONAL LOVE

NAMASKAR is an old East Indian proverb that says:

"LET ONLY THE GOOD IN ME SEE ONLY THE GOOD IN YOU."

Years ago, I made up my mind not to hate, but to try to love everyone. Unconditional love is difficult. The actions of some people are impossible to love. But remember that it is the actions of the person, not the person themselves.

Yes, there is that 2 percent of society, the diseased people who really need a lot of help understanding what is appropriate and what is not. In the cases of the people around us — our children, our partner, our friends — some things we can't understand. That does not mean we can not love them. When we go back to the teachings of Jesus, we understand when He talks about unconditional love.

LOVE THY NEIGHBOR AS THYSELF

Unconditional love takes the judgment out of relationships. It takes the hate out, the condemning out, the segregation out.

I don't care who you are. I don't care what you have done. I believe (contrary to some attitudes) that most people are inherently good. Most of us just want to be loved and accepted. Sometimes negative actions around us are just a call for love. Cut out this unnecessary step. Say to the people around you, "I love you. I believe in you. I trust you."

Love eliminates a lot of problems. So do trust and respect.

When I sold real estate, one colleague was known as a crook. His reputation was that he would steal a lead, or steal a deal.

One day, acting for a purchaser, I gave him an offer on one of his listings. I said I knew he would do a good job and that I trusted him to treat me fairly. He took the offer and the deal went through without a hitch.

If you pat a dog, the dog will wag its tail. If you hit it with a stick, it will growl.

UNDERSTAND AND ACCEPT
DIFFERENCES IN OTHERS

Judgments always bring conclusions. If someone doesn't believe what we believe, they are wrong.

Let us face facts. We all are different. We have different concepts. No two human beings are made exactly alike. No two human beings will feel exactly the same thing at exactly the same time. Understanding and accepting differences in others doesn't weaken our position. It makes us broader. It makes us wiser.

I've met some amazing people in my travels around the world. Often, the meeting has started out with criticism from me. "Look," I've thought. "He's coming toward me. Look at the way he's dressed. Look at the way he looks."

But underneath the shell of appearance, a wonderful soul often lurks.

One night job I had was in a group home for four mentally challenged seniors. Their differences, at first, were repulsive. My judgments got in the way. Once I got to know these four gentlemen, once I learned that how they walked and talked wasn't repulsive, just different, I understood they were simply people trying to get along in an imperfect world.

Not everyone thinks and believes as you do. We all are different. We have different looks, different ways of walking, talking, feeling, doing. Instead of condemning, instead of criticizing, try to understand. Realize we all are different and we have a right to our viewpoint.

WE HAVE A RIGHT TO BE
THE PEOPLE WE WERE MEANT TO BE
AS LONG AS WE DO NOT ADVERSELY AFFECT
THE PLANET OR ANY OTHER CREATURE IN IT

THE GOLDEN RULE

"Do unto others as you would have them do unto you." That old sawhorse. It's been around a long time. It's been said again and again. What startles me, what simply floors me, is the fact that hardly any of us live by the rules 100 percent. And you know that is what causes killings. That's what causes hatred. How could you hit someone if you don't want to be hit yourself? How could you steal from anybody if you don't want somebody to steal from you? How could you mentally abuse someone? Why would you call others names? Don't you remember how it hurt when someone called you names?

It is such a simple rule, this Golden Rule. "Do unto others as you would have them do to you." Does this empathy for others make too much sense?

Maybe so, but look at it this way: the Golden Rule is a short cut to personal happiness. If we choose to love all others unconditionally; if we choose to understand and accept differences in others; if we choose to treat all other people the way we'd like to be treated, life cannot help but offer spiritualism, balance and self worth.

I understand the fact that I am unique. There is no other Ted Mouradian on this earth. There is no other Ted Mouradian that feels what this Ted Mouradian feels. There is no other Ted Mouradian that can do what this Ted Mouradian does.

Once I realize and celebrate my uniqueness, then I also can celebrate the uniqueness of all others. Once I understand how I want to be treated, then I treat others the same way.

SPIRITUALISM AND RELIGION

When some people talk about spirituality, it somehow gets mixed in with religion. A spiritual person is not necessarily religious and a religious person is not necessarily spiritual. It seems to me that spiritualism came first and that religion and ritual sprang up around it as a way to standardize and legitimize this most personal experience. Boxing in spiritualism with rules and regulations is part of an obvious human need to contain and control, to limit, to package, to define.

I have some problems with religions and the interpretations of the teachings of the world's various prophets.

Over the last few years I have tried to understand the different types of religions of various cultures. Frankly, they confuse me. Most espouse the concept of love and the underlying need to care for neighbor and planet. In other words, each seeks similar goals and results. Why then do different religious sects use their specific teachings as a method of segregating, sometimes even destroying, those who do not believe in the same things they believe in. It is as if some are so insecure about who they are and what their religion stands for that they have to make sure no new ideas or concepts are taught in case they poke giant holes in their own religious structure. More wars have started and more people have died in the name of religion and God, than for any other reason.

My spiritual and religious beliefs, as I suspect of most of yours, were formed from the first contacts with this elusive thing.

As you already know, I am of Armenian heritage. Armenians are Christians and the religion is Orthodox. As a child, I went to Sunday school. I participated in Christmas and Easter pageants. I sang in the church choir. I was an altar boy assisting the priest during service.

My head was filled with God and Jesus while all around me people were poor, or dying or being mistreated. Unanswered questions bubbled from within. I was told that if someone didn't believe the same things "we" believed in, we should not talk to them or we should try to convert them to "our" way of thinking. I was told things that felt good, were sinful. Things that looked bad, but were done in the name of God, I was told were OK. My belief seemed lost in chaos. Tradition seemed more important than reality. Habit suffocated inquiry.

Here's a crutch. "If the church says it is so, it must be right." So easy. So comfortable. So dangerous.

WHY THE CARVER CARVES

There is an old story of a young man who watched his father remove a roast from the oven on Thanksgiving. The ends of the roast were cut off. So the young man questioned his father for the reason. His father thought a moment but couldn't give the reason. He said his mother cut the ends off the roast.

So, he asked his mother why. She said she too was taught by her mother and her mother always cut off the ends of the roast. They went to the den.

"Grandma, why do you cut the ends off the roast?" he asked.

"Interesting question," she said. "My mother always cut the ends off the roast. That's what I was taught and that's what I taught your mother."

They went to Great-Grandma's room and ask why she cut the ends off the roast.

She looked up and said, "Well, back in my time, the pans were too small."

The parallel with religion can be supported with any number of examples. But the point is that we still do things that were appropriate 2000 years ago but are not valid today. We condemn and judge others for reasons no longer justified as we enter the 21st century.

This isn't a call to arms. It is an appeal to you to stop and question. Think about your habitual actions. Ask yourself why you do the things you do. Do you cut the ends off roasts without knowing why?

When there were too many questions without answers, I abandoned any religion or sect that has killed, discriminated or persecuted anyone who did not believe what they believed.

"But wait," you say. "I belong to a religious group. I believe in God and Jesus, but I don't condone everything my church says or does."

I say that if you don't like what is going on, try to change it. Inaction against other parishioners committing wrongful acts in the name of YOUR God, makes you just as guilty.

I understand that the dogma of religion is weighty, the issue is extremely large. But listen to Pastor Martin Niemolloer:

"IN GERMANY THEY FIRST CAME FOR THE COMMUNISTS AND I DIDN'T SPEAK UP BECAUSE I WAS NOT A COMMUNIST. THEN THEY CAME FOR THE JEWS AND I DIDN'T SPEAK UP BECAUSE I WASN'T A JEW. THEN THEY CAME FOR THE TRADE UNIONISTS AND I DIDN'T SPEAK UP BECAUSE I WASN'T A TRADE UNIONIST. THEY CAME FOR THE CATHOLICS AND I DIDN'T SPEAK UP BECAUSE I WAS A PROTESTANT. THEN THEY CAME FOR ME AND BY THAT TIME THERE WAS NO ONE LEFT TO SPEAK UP."

Think about these words. Think about the wars, the persecutions, the denials. We can not just stand by any longer. GOD IS LOVE! Unconditional love. That's it. We must stand up for peace and understanding. It starts with the individual. Unity will come when we learn to accept the differences in others and allow them to be the persons they were meant to be.

EVERYONE SHOULD BE ALLOWED TO DO AND BE WHO THEY WERE MEANT TO BE AS LONG AS THEY ARE NOT ADVERSELY AFFECTING THE PLANET OR ANYONE ON IT

The heart of the matter is that spiritualism is an evolving entity. Growth comes from challenge and meeting challenges from a foundation of basic beliefs. Security in a spiritual belief system allows for questioning, examining and exploring other concepts without being threatened in any way. I feel very strongly about the concept of oneness with the planet and every living creature.

Here is a chant that will help focus on the concept of oneness:

I AM ONE WITH THE SPIRIT
I AM ONE WITH MYSELF
I AM ONE WITH THE HUMAN FAMILY
I AM ONE WITH ALL LIVING THINGS
I AM ONE WITH THE PLANET
I AM ONE WITH THE UNIVERSE

Sit tall with legs crossed and take three deep, slow breaths. Then repeat the above three times in full each day.

I think that if we can understand and accept the differences in others and learn to live harmoniously with all others we will be able to do away with war, killing, stealing, anger and hate. Of course, total compassion isn't around the next corner. It starts with the individual, one piece (or peace) at a time. If we're able to center and balance ourselves, no one and no thing can hurt us except ourselves.

Native people are an outstanding example. They believe that all of creation is interconnected, that we are all part of a single organism. Because of this, what happens in one circumstance ultimately affects another. They also believe that we are all the children of Mother Earth and we must respect her for once she is destroyed there is no life. We all turn to Mother Earth for everything we need to survive. Therefore, the importance of looking after her and her inhabitants is self evident.

My beliefs are similar. The book *Three Magic Words* by U.S. Anderson has helped me put them in words. Anderson talks about a Universal Subconscious Mind and his belief that we are all connected by energy. He says all creation and the creation of anything is a result of thought, and thought comes from the subconscious mind.

Because I believe I am interconnected with everything and every being on this planet, why would I want to hurt myself? Why would I want to maim myself? Why would I want to lie to myself? Why would I want to destroy myself? If we can believe this concept of interconnection, if we can believe this energy force is in us, around us and beside us, then why would we want to destroy who we are?

If I look for the best in others and if I give the best I can give to any situation, I find the initial effort is rewarded by less stressful days and better sleeps at night.

I call this balance. I also use the terms: oneness with the planet, centered, one with the self, connected to the Universal Subconscious Mind.

BALANCE

Balance is like a free-spinning wheel, free of friction, if you will. When I am out of balance, the wheel wobbles. Spokes are missing. We can recognize there are forces out there that can cause our wheel to be unbalanced but it is up to us to put our wheel back in balance.

Keeping balanced is not an easy task. It is hard work and takes great concentration. I, too, lose my balance from time to time. But the more I try, the less frequent it becomes. And the wheel wobbles less each time.

MIND, BODY AND SPIRIT

The mind, body and spirit are one. Not separate. One. Without strong spirituality, the mind is weak. If the mind is weak, the body suffers. If the body suffers, the spirit is broken.

Disconnection from the spiritual world around us brings rootlessness. Without foundation as a person, we have low self-esteem. It manifests itself as job tension, relationship tension, personal anxiety. Then it turns on the body. Without the original energy force, we wind up with ulcers, nervous tension, high blood pressure, heart disease.

We must let go and trust the spirit. Trust the self. Call it what you will. God. Goddess. Buddha. Allah. The Universal Subconscious. Call it the Self. This energy exists. It is part of us and it is part of all living creatures.

It seems, at first, a hard stretch to blame physical discomfort or illness on a lack of spirituality. It is abstract and it manifests itself as trust in our own intuition. When we're in touch with the deepest part of ourselves, we instinctively make the right choices. The feeling says, "This is the way to turn. This is good. This is right. This is the way things should be."

Then we can let go. We can lose our inhibitions in the strength of the spirit. When you trust that force, you realize nothing and no one can hurt you, except you. This happens only when you go against the direction you're guiding your self.

Again, some things beyond personal control can throw you off course. It is your reaction to those things that determines the quality of life you have. Your reaction is how you once again, regain your balance.

If the sprit is deep, the mind is peaceful. If the mind is at peace, the body is strong. A strong body brings peace of mind. Peace of mind opens the heart to the spirit. This is the continuum between body, spirit and mind.

One day, I lost a speaking contract because the company couldn't get funding. Organizers of a speech two days forward announced I wouldn't be paid for a month. My mother took an overdose of pills. (She is OK). That evening, I made a scheduled dinner speech. I wasn't thrown off kilter by the events earlier. I was balanced. My speech received a standing ovation and my success there has probably led to enough new work to make up for all the lost money. It didn't do anything for my mother, unfortunately. Balance, for her, seems to be the enemy, although every day she keeps trying and trying.

Spirit, mind and body are one. The first signs of illness, for me, are the first signs that there is something I must work out. I feel meditative. I sit and try to figure out what is really causing the trouble. I ask, "What caused this unbalance?" I look to my relationships, because everything we do and everything that affects us is the result of our relationship with ourselves, with others or with this planet.

Once I figure out the cause of this loss of balance, I deal with it. If it is with myself, I determine where I stopped being true to myself and re-orient my focus. If it has to do with a person, then I go to that person and correct whatever happened. Often, when I outline my anguish, my antagonist says they didn't even realize what they did would affect me adversely.

If my problem has somehow put a wedge between me and the planet, I go outdoors, to the source. The beauty of earth is a great healer. Time is the best medicine. For every moment invested in the well being of the planet, peace is returned tenfold.

Again, if we have a good strong spiritual feeling, that harmony brings us peace and tranquillity. If we trust the spirit, then our mind is free. If our mind is free and our mind is light, then the illnesses that affect the body are fewer and farther between.

As I put this sentence down, I am in my 45th year. Most people peg me in my mid-30s. I don't feel 45, whatever 45 is supposed to feel like. I suspect my younger appearance has much to do with balance and the removal of pressures from my life.

Even when life "does it" to me, even when something adverse enters my sphere of happiness, I take it for what it is. "This moment is as it should be," is an oft-repeated saying. I'll go a step farther. The moment is as it is. It's use is for learning. We learn from the journey, one step at a time.

ASK "WHY?"

If the first step to balance is connecting spirit, mind and body, the second step is filled with questions.

In any situation, we need to know why we are doing what we are doing. Ask yourself, "Why am I doing this?" Ask often and answer honestly.

Asking this question, puts us in control of the situations we are in. If I know why I sit where I sit, why I set my office the way it is, why I dress the way I dress, why I say the things I do, then I can understand why I react the way I do.

As I've said, we can't control everything that happens to us. But we can control our reactions. So knowing why we react a certain way improves those reactions. This refinement leads us closer and closer to the balance we seek.

Pretend you're on a two-lane highway. Traffic is light but cars ahead of you have boxed you in. You catch them and frustration mounts quickly. You edge up until you are almost riding the bumper of the one in the faster lane. The car doesn't speed up or move over. Even though its doing the speed limit, the rules of the road say the driver should surrender the lane to the faster car. That's you. Instead, you must sit and fume.

Or must you?

Here is a situation you can't control, but your reaction can be patience or impatience. Ask yourself, "Why is it so frustrating? Is it that driver's belligerence?" All your anger can't change that attitude. What if you are fuming and you have yet to be noticed?

Why are you speeding anyway? If you are in a hurry, accept the consequences of leaving too late.

Why is it that we so often ruin the journey for the sake of the destination?

By asking the question "why" as often as possible, we'll likely find that our stress is self-inflicted, that it comes from our perception of situations. Usually, our answers aren't even related to a current incident or situation.

Think of the highway scenario. Is the driver ahead of you the object of frustration that belongs to another relationship?

The objective is to understand why you do what you do, then to tailor your reactions to best keep in harmony your spirit, mind and body.

For myself, I now understand why I don't like certain events or don't want to associate with certain types of personalities. I fully understand why I take on a certain belief system. I try to listen to my spirit, mind and body. I used to eat at certain times of the day because that is what I was programmed to do. Breakfast at 8. Lunch at noon. Dinner at 6. Now I listen to my body. I eat when I'm hungry. And I eat the foods that my body tells me to eat, not necessarily the foods someone says I should eat. If I was thirsty, I used to just drink. Now I know why I drink. My body needs water. Why three glasses? That is what my body asked for.

Remember to keep asking yourself, "Why are you cutting the ends off the roast? Why am I fuming at a driver who doesn't see me behind him?"

Once we realize why we do what we do, the things we do have meaning and become more worthwhile, more valuable. It adds clarity to our actions.

PERCEPTION

I've touched only briefly on perception, but recognizing point of view is another way to combat what knocks us off balance. Someone might say, "Ted, you are gross." Early in my life, the comment would have been like an arrow to my heart. Now I know I'm not gross and can say, "If that's what you think, so be it."

Each of us perceives life a certain way.

Picture an old train in Europe, with four people in a compartment:

The passengers were an old General, a prim, proper, mature and stately woman, a beautiful young woman and a young Corporal.

The train went through a tunnel. It was pitch black and no one could see a thing. There was a loud kiss, then a hard slap. When the train came out of the tunnel, the General was rubbing the side of his face with his hand.

"Well, isn't that interesting," he thought. "The young man tried to kiss the young woman, she thought it was me and slapped me. Oh well, people make mistakes."

The mature woman sitting next to the General said to herself, "Hmmm. That old general tried to kiss the young woman. Good for her. She kept her virtue and slapped him."
The young woman, sitting next to the mature woman, thought to herself, "Isn't that fun that the old general tried to kiss the woman. Good for her. She kept her

virtue and slapped him. It's nice to see they are still active at that age."

The young Corporal barely contained himself. "Ha, ha, ha," he laughed. "I kissed the back of my hand and slapped that old general across the face and nobody knew I did it."

Perception, more than we might expect, rules our lives. I can perceive I'll have a bad day. Guess what? I will have a bad day. If I perceive I'll have a good day, I will have a good day. If I'm in a strange area, I can perceive I'll be robbed or will have a bad time or that someone will take advantage of me. It will happen.

Everyone, of course, is entitled to their perceptions. We each have our own. The one problem I have with perceptions is when people take their own point of view to adversely affect someone else. We must ask why. "Why do you see this, this way? Why do we see bad in this person? Why is this a difficult situation?" Asking these questions will usually change these perceptions. Altering perceptions for the better makes life that much better.

Try once to wake up in the morning and decide life is wonderful. Perceive everyone you meet will enhance your day. Even if it is dull out, the sun is shining somewhere, and that somewhere is in the heart of the optimist.

It is very difficult to be out of balance when you are perceiving so much goodness and happiness in all of the people and all of the situations you are in. With proper perception, you can remain in balance and strengthen a great spiritual relationship.

ACCEPTANCE IS NOT NECESSARILY AGREEMENT

Conflict ruins balance. Conflict comes from trying to change others or trying to change yourself for others. Just as common a conflict is an argument over a simple point of view. But conflict over change is worse. It originates from deeper within. Therefore, any solution to that conflict must also be found at that depth.

But here's a thought to relieve the pressure of both conflicts. Acceptance is not necessarily agreement.

> EVERYONE IS ALLOWED TO BE THE PERSON
> THEY WERE MEANT TO BE AS LONG
> AS THEY DON'T ADVERSELY AFFECT
> THE PLANET OR ANYONE ON IT

This short saying takes much of the fight from our sails.

Each of us is different. Customs and beliefs are not necessarily right or wrong. People who harm no one else have a right to be left alone.

We must accept, but not necessarily agree, with those who have different views than us.

The idea is to let go. Live and let live. If I accept you, I am not judging you. If I am not judging you, then I don't have to worry about being judged.

It's a wonderful way to live — free of guilt and free of the burden of trying to change everyone or every moment.

Maintaining balance is not an easy job. It takes constant monitoring. But there is a pace to the life of balanced people, a satisfying cadence, a dance those without the rhythm can only envy.

Balance is a holistic look at life. It requires proper diet, adequate exercise, enough work and enough play. If all your senses are enhanced in a positive manner, then you can not help but to stay balanced.

Remember the concept of Yin and Yang. "In all good there is some bad and in all bad there is some good." I always look for and concentrate on the good knowing there will be bad. So, when bad happens, it doesn't seem so terrible.

There is a lesson in good times and bad. We can question why rotten things happen to us. We can point a finger, find a scapegoat, blame others. Or we can use all of our experiences for what they are; experiences, life experiences. Hopefully, it makes us better people when we can learn from these experiences. We are here to learn. Those who learn, advance. Those who don't, keep repeating the same lessons.

IT IS NOT WHAT HAPPENS TO US
IN LIFE THAT COUNTS.
IT IS WHAT WE DO ABOUT IT

My idea is always that nothing is wrong, that no one is really all bad. I try not to take things that happen as a personal affront. I do get angry. I do get disappointed. I'm not always balanced but I continue to work for this equilibrium. I try to determine what is the bottom line and what is really happening. In most instances I find that I am not hurt physically. If I am hurt mentally, it is the way I am perceiving the situation.

Introspection is awareness.

The more I concentrate on being balanced and centered, the more I walk without blinders, the more synchronized I become with the planet and the people around me.

Success and failure, happiness and sadness, flows from the state of balance and imbalance.

When life "does it" to you:
- Ask yourself: "What is the bottom line? Will I die? Will I lose my house? Will I lose a friend?"
- Is it worth getting upset over?
- Why, really, am I angry? Does it relate to unconnected incidents?

When life "does it" to you:
- Think things through before you act or react.
- Put your troubles in perspective. Things can always get worse — and BETTER.

THE NUMBER OF PEOPLE AT YOUR FUNERAL WILL DEPEND ON WHETHER IT RAINS THAT DAY

We can worry so much about our mortality, that we can completely miss the journey from birth to death. We are so concerned about what people think of us and how they'll remember us that we don't live for ourselves and our contentment. We hoard things to leave behind a legacy and miss out on using them in life.

Take a close look at a coffin. There are no drawers. Whatever you've collected, it's not coming with you. Spread it around and see what good it does. Do things to be remembered today, not to be remembered at your funeral.

Things decay, but deeds live forever! Whether living or dead, you have no control over the weather at your funeral.

THE ONLY COMMODITY WE HAVE IN LIFE IS TIME

If you were given a bank account with a balance of $86,400 and were told: "Don't bother trying to save the money. Whatever you don't spend in the next 24 hours will be taken back." I'll bet that money would be spent carefully and fully. Knowing you have only that one chance would make you consider your purchases to make the most out of that one-time offering.

Guess what. We all have that type of account. But the currency isn't dollars, it's time. We're given 86,400 seconds a day to spend any way we want. We can't save them. We can't hoard them. All we can do is spend those seconds the best way we can.

With money, most of us are very careful. We check it and safeguard it and protect it against theft. Not so with time. Today, I bet, you could recall a moment when someone was allowed to steal your time. You've even squandered it yourself, thinking about someone or something that was out of your control, that, regardless of the amount of pondering, would not change. You were robbed of that time in collusion with the person that took so much thought. The funny thing is you didn't even know you were an accessory.

Just like a bank account in your name, only you can control how your time is drawn. Happiness is a decision. Don't let anyone take that away. Spend each day, spend each hour, spend each minute as if it were precious gold. Time, in fact, is more valuable than gold. It is your life.

(OMMIT YOURSELF TO LIFE

We spend a lot of time just putting in time. We're here in life, in body, but not mind. We miss a lot. Do you remember your drive to work today or did you arrive and practically forget how you got there?

When was the last time you were so preoccupied that a loved one's question received a mumble in reply? Later, did you ask them the same question?

Have you ever looked at a new building on one of your regular routes and asked yourself, "When did they build that?"

We're busy, busy people. We have so much going on in our little brains that we can't seem to concentrate on the now. But yesterday is gone. Decisions were made, actions taken. Yesterday is done and we can't take it back. Tomorrow is still beyond the horizon. Except for preservation of our well being, and the cause and effect of our actions, we don't need to worry about the unknown. Live for the moment. Right actions today spawn right actions tomorrow. If we savor each second we're given, if we commit to the now, we'll make each moment worth remembering.

Commitment to now, thinking about where we are and what we are doing, brings fewer mistakes and fewer accidents. See the trees, then the forest.

CAFÉ AU LAIT

There was café in St. Catharines I liked to frequent (and where most of this book was written). One day I was sitting at a table for two in a section where the tables can be joined to accommodate larger parties. This is a difficult feat in the rest of the café. Anyway, a family of six arrived speaking broken English. They searched for a place to sit and ended up at three tables for two. I moved so they could join some tables and sit together.

Had I not been observing the environment, had I been wrapped up in myself, I would have missed the opportunity to help, to make their day a little nicer. No big deal. No great reward. It felt good though, and hopefully those six people will remember the act (not me) and do the same for someone else someday.

BACK TO THE NOW

Committing to the now allows you to share your whole self with yourself and the people around you. Commitment to the now brings wonders that have eluded you in the past. Committing to the now fills life with new adventure and joy.

Walk to the garbage can. Unhook those horse blinders.

Throw them away. Commit to the now and see things in their proper perspective.

Sure, plan for the future, but let the future evolve from the now. The future doesn't just start up.

If we constantly worry about and dream of our destination, we'll miss the journey. And, in life, the journey is what is important.

LIGHTEN UP, WILL YOU?

Laugh at stress. Laugh at difficulties. Shame them to their proper size and position. Stress, difficulty, hardship they don't rule your life. They infringe on your ability to rule your life. They aren't beasts, they're bugs. So scale them back to their proper perspective.

Humor can be the best medicine. Very serious doctors have made studies that show humor relieves stress, that a happy frame of mind helps the healing process. Laugh your way out of difficulty.

Perhaps constant good moods will confuse friends who think it isn't appropriate to find humor in everything. I even agree that certain times and situations call for sadness, even anger. But sullenness, that's something different altogether.

Indeed, good moods simply come from how we look at life and how we relate ourselves to any given situation. Look on the "Light Side". There's good in most situations. Seeing the good, or perhaps just not being mired in the bad, usually brings out humor.

RUNNING ON EMPTY

I had made a luncheon appointment with a friend, a prominent interior designer in St. Catharines. She wanted to do some presentations on empowerment and was looking for some advice.

The lunch was set for a Tuesday noon. On Monday she requested a delay until 12:30 p.m. It would put me slightly behind schedule but I agreed.

I picked her up in my car. I was low on gas but figured we could make it to the nearby town of Niagara-on-the-Lake. I entered the highway, eyes on the gas gauge. As we passed a restaurant and tennis club, my friend suggested we eat there. I took the next exit, came around the cloverleaf and sputtered to a stop, out of gas on the off ramp.

We laughed. I said to wait and listen to the radio while I went for fuel. I stuck out my thumb and the first car gave me a ride. I got the gas and started back hoping no one I knew would see me.

I was seen. A small black car pulled up alongside. It was Alan Simmons, another professional speaker, who happens to live in Peterborough, Ontario, quite a distance away. He said he was driving to Niagara-on-the-Lake later that day and had tried to contact me for lunch.

Of all the people to meet. Alan is the person I have gone to for advice on speaking and my friend wanted advice on speaking. It turned out to be a great lunch and beneficial to all concerned.

This small story offers some simple advice. Don't take disruptive events too seriously. The journey of life is what counts. Put events in their proper perspective, as a small piece in the tapestry of your life.

Running out of gas turned out to be a good thing. Maybe things aren't going the way you planned, but they are still going. Maybe the new route will be better.

THE HELPING HAND HELPS ITSELF

Think back, if you can, to when you were learning to walk. When you fell, someone was there to help you up. Remember that person.

Remember your first days of school. You were frightened and someone came up and said, "You're new here. So am I. Let's help each other."

In school, when you went out to the playground, remember the person who approached you and said, "Let's be friends," and how they helped you?

Remember your first forays into sports or a new group. You were frightened and alone. Someone came up and said, "First time? Well, I can show you the ropes." Remember that person.

Remember your first job. Remember the person who eased your trepidation and went out of their way to help you adjust.

Remember all the people who over the years helped you get where you are today or were there for you when you needed them. Remember the helping hand.

Stop asking, "What's in it for me?"

One day, Jack and Humphry were burdened by packs on their backs. They were very tired, but had to go on to the next town. They were resting by the side of the road, wondering how they would carry their loads, when an old sage drove by.

She had a wagon, and two strong horses. And the wagon was only half full.

"Those look like heavy loads," she said to Humphry and Jack. "I have room, and two strong horses. Load your packs with me and I'll take them as far as I'm going."

Humphry beamed. Jack was suspicious. "What's in it for you?" he demanded. "What do you want?"

"I saw a long way back you needed a helping hand," the sage said. "What do I want? For repayment, I ask that when you see someone else who needs a helping hand, help and ask for nothing in return. Then you can consider your debt repaid."

In the bible, the Good Samaritan is never named. It doesn't matter what his name was.

It is your opinion of yourself that matters most, not recognition from others.

Each event in our life is the result of our relationship with ourselves, others and the planet.

We manage our relationships by choosing how we react to each event.

Correct reaction stems from an inner balance of spirit, mind and body.

Inner balance brings harmony to our relationship with ourselves, others and the planet.

So:
- Be reliable in everything you do.
- Go through life with dignity.
- Master your own destiny.
- Walk softly to reach goals. Don't leave a path of destruction in your wake.

On your new journey and in each step of the way, I wish you all the **BEST IN LIFE**.

> — TED MOURADIAN, 1997
> St. Catharines, Ontario

THE JOURNEY CONTINUES ...

A JOURNEY BEGINS

The decision is made and
I am strangely at peace with it.
I plunge myself into an uncertain destiny,
yet my fear is not all consuming.

I arrange my thoughts for the sake
of clarity, so that I may know
each step as I take it, even
though the path I walk is unknown.

Fear aside, I am empowered to seize
this day and all others that follow.
They are mine to have, to shape, to share,
to give away, and to take.
I alone have the answers.
I alone have the desire.

My journey has a pace that consists of
long comfortable strides; more fluid,
more graceful than before.
There is beauty in what I do
A confidence to my actions
A direction to my thoughts.

I am not afraid

— Troy A. Brooks
   February 6, 1997

THE RELATIONSHIP WRAP UP

- You will be free to be the person you were meant to be once you allow all others to be free to be the people they were meant to be.
- Being different is not wrong
- Learn who you are and what you need.
- Be reliable.
- Treat everyone with respect.
- Understand that we all have baggage.
- Accept that everyone is entitled to take their own journey.
- The only commodity we have in life is time.
- Be spontaneous.
- Do not leave a path of destruction in your wake.
- See the good in everyone and everything.
- Leave people with a good feeling.
- Respect all life.
- Respect our planet.
- Accept differences in others.
- Stop violent or controlling behavior.
- Educate, don't segregate.
- Lighten up.
- Keep life simple.
- Help others.
- Enjoy your journey.
- To feel is to live.
- Laugh a lot. Hug a lot.
- To live is to feel.

To inquire about Ted Mouradian and Humphry the Camel's seminars, meeting planning and consulting, call or write to:

THE HUMPHRY GROUP
P.O. BOX 671
ST. CATHARINES ON L2R 6W8
CANADA

Phone: (905) 682-7380
Fax: (905) 682-1501
E-mail: humphry@iaw.on.ca

Maritimes•Arts•Projects•Productions *a selection of publications*

ISBN	Author/Title	Imprint	$ Unit
0-921411-63-4	Acorn, Milton. **Reading from** *More Poems for People*.(C-45) ✉	SpareTime	9.95
0-919957-63-3	Blades, Joe. **Solstice.**	SpareTime	2.95
0-919957-60-9	Blades, Joe. **Cover Makes a Set.** ✉	SpareTime	8.95
0-919957-61-7	Blades, Joe. **future now past.**	SpareTime	3.95
0-919957-64-1	Blades, Joe. **Stones of My Flesh.**	SpareTime	2.95
0-921411-27-8	Blades, Joe. **Synopsis.**	Book Rat	3.95
0-921411-39-1	Blades, Joe (ed) **may contain and/or**	DSPP	3.95
0-921411-62-6	Blades, Joe (ed). **In the Dark— Poets & Publishing**	BJP	7.95
0-921411-24-3	Bull, Arthur; Bull, Ruth (ill.) **Hawthorn.**	BJP	4.95
0-921411-30-8	Deahl, James. **Under The Watchful Eye: Poetry and Discourse** ✉	BJP	11.95
0-921411-32-4	Deahl, James; Fitzgerald, D.C. **Poetry and Music from** *Under The Watchful Eye* (C-60 cassette). ✉	BJP	11.95
0-921411-26-X	flaming, p.j. **voir dire.** ✉	BJP	11.95
0-921411-28-6	Folsom, Eric. **Poems for Little Cataraqui.** ✉	BJP	10.95
0-921411-38-3	Footman, Jennifer (ed.) **An Invisible Accordion.** ✉	BJP	14.95
0-921411-45-6	Footman, Jennifer. **St Valentine's Day.** ✉	BJP	13.95
0-921411-54-5	Gates, Edward. **There Are No Limits to How Far the Traveller Can Go**	BJP	3.95
0-921411-36-7	Gibbs, Robert. **Earth Aches.**	BJP	2.95
0-921411-41-3	Hawkes, Robert. **This Grievous Injury.**	BJP	2.95
0-921411-50-2	Iskov, I.B. **Anxiety Attack.**	BJP	3.95
0-921411-13-8	Jankola, Beth. **Drawings by Poet.**	BJP	5.95
0-921411-40-5	LeDuc, M.R. **Reflections of a Frog.**	BJP	3.95
0-921411-51-0	MacDonald, Shane. **Diary of a Broken Heart.**	BJP	2.95
0-921411-47-2	Madsen, Alex. **Thoughts Organized & Otherwise,** vol 1.	BJP	4.95
0-921411-34-0	mclennan, rob. **Poems from the Blue Horizon.**	BJP	3.95
0-921411-55-3	Mouradian, Ted. **Best in Life.** ✉	MAPP	17.95
0-921411-33-2	Pieroway, Phyllis. **Memories of Sandy Point, St George's Bay Newfoundland.** ✉	MAPP	14.95
0-921411-46-4	Pieroway, Charles Warren. **Sandy Point Map.**	MAPP	4.95
0-921411-51-0	Redekopp, Jean. **A View from the Bucket.** ✉	MAPP	14.95
0-921411-25-1	Richards, David Adams. **A Lad from Brantford** ✉	BJP	11.95
0-921411-37-5	Schmidt, Tom. **The Best Lack All.** ✉	BJP	12.95
0-921411-29-4	Smith, Diana. **Ripples from the Phoenix.**	MAPP	2.95
0-921411-22-7	Trakl, Georg; Skelton, Robin (trans.) **Dark Seasons.** ✉	BJP	10.95
0-921411-44-8	Vaughan, R M. **The InCorrupt Tables.**	BJP	2.95
0-921411-11-1	Wendt, Karl. **Chaste Wood.** ✉	BJP	7.95
ISSN 0840-4747	**New Muse of Contempt** magazine (One year subscription)	MPP	8.00

* Unit prices listed (excluding the *New Muse of Contempt* subscription) do not include GST/HST taxes. Our Revenue Canada number is 12489 7943 RT****

Ask your local bookseller to order our publications from General Distribution Services, 30 Lesmilles Rd, Don Mills ON M3B 2T6: phone Toronto 416 445-3333; Ontario/Quebec 1-800-387-0141; rest of Canada 1-800-387-0172; USA 1-800-805-1083. For a full catalogue, or to order direct from the publisher, write to our address below. Individual orders must be prepaid with cheque or money order. Please add $2 shipping for the first ✉ marked item ordered and/or 50¢ per additional item.

All Canadian orders must add 7% GST/HST to the total dollar value of publications plus 15% HST to postage/shipping.

We cannot accept credit card orders.

Maritimes Arts Projects Productions
BOX 506 STN A
FREDERICTON NB E3B 5A6
CANADA

Ph/fax: 506 454-5127
E-mail: jblades@nbnet.nb.ca